50 NOT OUT!

Powerful Life Lessons from Cricket to Excel in Our Lives

Harimohan Paruvu

W0006091

JAICO PUBLISHING HOUSE

Ahmedabad Bangalore Bhopal Bhubaneswar Chennai
Delhi Hyderabad Kolkata Lucknow Mumbai

Published by Jaico Publishing House
A-2 Jash Chambers, 7-A Sir Phirozshah Mehta Road
Fort, Mumbai - 400 001
jaicopub@jaicobooks.com
www.jaicobooks.com

50 NOT OUT!
ISBN 978-81-8495-657-3

First Jaico Impression: 2016
Second Jaico Impression: 2017

Printed by
SAP Print Solutions Pvt. Ltd.
28 A, Laxmi Industrial Estate, S. N. Path
Lower Parel (W), Mumbai - 400 013

What do they know of cricket who only cricket know?
– CLR James

To my mother who, without understanding what this game was about, encouraged me wholeheartedly to play it merely because I loved it. And in doing so, exemplified one of the greatest principles that life teaches us: Giving unconditional support to those you love.

And the game of cricket, for being one of the greatest teachers I have ever had.

CONTENTS

ACKNOWLEDGEMENTS

I WOULD LIKE TO EXPRESS my gratitude to the many people who saw me through this book:

The game of cricket first. All the cricketers who played with me and against me and taught me through their every act. All the heroes we admired and tried to emulate. All the coaches and teachers who have tried to instill these principles in us as we learned to deal with the world. All the teams – my family plays a big part, my galli teams, my schools, my colleges, my universities, my employers, the Hyderabad Cricket Association and the BCCI – who have actively supported my learning through the game. A big part is owed to cricket writers and commentators who have made the game interesting.

Sudeshna Shome Ghosh, for giving me the idea for this book. Keerti Ramachandra, always the first to hear my ideas, for believing they had enough steam and working on the tough initial drafts. Vidyuth Jaisimha, one of my first readers on all things cricket, and whose cricketing knowledge I respect highly, for reading the first draft and supporting me fully as he always does. Vivek Jaisimha, who has been the big brother, a big part of my growth as a cricketer and one with astute knowledge of the game. Venkatapathy Raju, who has shared many stories with me in addition to sharing kit bags, railway berths and rooms on tours. Rehmat Baig, who remains a dedicated coach, one of the heroes I look up to and a coach with the most passion ever. Bro. Joseph, who is such a delight to know and discuss anything under the sun with, but chiefly cricket and education. Friends Rajesh Janwadkar, Vijay Devarakonda and Vijay Purushottaman Nair, who read initial drafts and gave their views from the corporate perspective. Vinod Ekbote, for giving me wholesome writerly advice and keeping me in good humour. They have all read and contributed to this book.

I have quoted from various sources, books, movies, incidents and cannot say how much they have influenced my thoughts. Vijay Mohan Raj, Sunil Joshi, Noel David and Srinivas Avasarala, for sharing their life experiences readily. Many cricketer friends who have shared their time and knowledge with me. My team members at the Marredpally Cricket Club, who facilitated so much learning. Bosses, colleagues and customers who have demonstrated that cricketing principles can be applied to life. Friends and clients Rama Raju and Suresh Reddy, among other clients of mine, who have encouraged me to share these cricketing principles in corporate training sessions and workshops. Surendra Chacha for designing the icons at short notice. Tarun Chauhan, for adding a delectable touch in the end.

The team at Jaico, Sandhya Iyer for believing in my idea and Akash Shah for supporting it. Sabine Algur, for being a wonderful editor and adding tremendous value to the book, taking it to a level I could not have on my own. Much is owed to them.

My big family, which finds great joy in my little achievements and makes me feel very special. My brother Ram, for being my earliest teammate while playing the game and for always standing like a rock behind me. My wife Shobha, who quietly supports me in my growth, which involves several crazy decisions. My daughter Anjali, who speeds up my growth process rapidly with her unbounded enthusiasm and joie de vivre (and some plain speaking).

This book would not have been possible without you all.

PREFACE

50 NOT OUT! is my attempt at compiling some of the lessons that cricket taught me. I learned them over a period of time and have applied them to my life. When I look around, I find that others have also applied these principles successfully in all walks of life, and it makes me feel that I am on a good wicket. Playing cricket has not been a waste of time at all.

As a young cricketer, I was intrigued at the practices and techniques that the game demanded of us. Clearly, those who understood and followed these mysterious practices fared better as cricketers. Some terms made sense to me, while others did not. As I grew older and interacted with some of the knowledgeable practitioners of the game, I realized that there was much more to the game than just what I was doing; so many of the finer points were missing. Every match taught me a new lesson and left a question in my mind.

When I started working in the corporate sector,

I found that many of these cricketing principles were applicable in the work environment, too. Many of those I applied at work have been shared here. Evidently, the popular cricketing phrases we hear so often on television have far greater value and insight.

After my professional playing days were over, I continued to be part of the Sunday league games for Marredpally Cricket Club, just to see how these principles would work – how to design a win, how to get the team working together, how to get the best out of our resources, how to lead and how to follow, etc. When I reflected on it, I could see what I did right or wrong. Cricket gives instant feedback.

I believe that this book could be a fun way to understand the game and also benefit from it. Whether you are preparing for success, dealing with people, uncertainty or stress – knowing your cricket helps. In fact, in one of my roles as an executive coach to senior executives, I help them seek solutions to corporate situations through cricketing principles, tactics and strategies. I use the cricketing analogy extensively in talks, workshops and training sessions.

Having said that, I must also say what *50 Not Out!* is not. It is an easy read, not an academic exercise and there is no attempt to make it serious reading beyond what the reader may perceive. The content is limited to my experience and knowledge and bits and pieces of history, which have been verified only by the most cursory of research. If anything must be taken seriously, it is the lesson or the principle and its application, evaluated and adapted by the reader.

My deeper purpose at writing these lessons is to further glorify this lovely game, which has now made its way into the hearts of people of all ages, groups and genders, and to show its many wonderful shades from different perspectives. More than anything, this book is a celebration of the game. Any learning emanating from it is a complete bonus for the reader.

1 | COURAGE

"I learned that courage was not the absence of fear, but the triumph over it. The brave man is not he who does not feel afraid, but he who conquers that fear." – Nelson Mandela

Get behind the line of the ball.

THE CRICKET BALL is not a friendly red cherry. Give it to a fast bowler and the five-and-a-half ounce ball comes cannoning towards your body at speeds of over a 140 kmph, carrying with it the promise of bruising your flesh, spilling your blood, breaking your bones and even killing you. It is the reason why facing fast bowling ranks among the most unpleasant aspects of the game of cricket. But even as every instinct, thought and emotion urges you to flee, you have to find a way to deal with it. Not surprisingly, the prescribed technique to play fast bowling is to get in line with the ball. When in line, the batsman has a clear line of sight which enables him to deal with the ball appropriately – defend, attack or leave alone. Batsmen who run away from the ball towards the square leg are dead meat. Word gets around.

Watching the best players face fast bowling helps us to understand this aspect better. Sunil Gavaskar, for one, because he faced the quickest and meanest bowlers the world had ever produced without the comfort of a helmet on pitches that were not batsmen friendly. Watch Gavaskar step into line fearlessly, and hook bouncers from Andy Roberts bowling around the stumps, or weave away from a nasty, rising ball whizzing inches from his nose and you know exactly why he averages 65.45 against the vicious West Indian attacks. He will not back off and will always get in line! He will stand up and face the unpleasantness and the hostility.

Former Indian Test cricketer and now television commentator Ravi Shastri recalls an incident involving Sunil Gavaskar and the West Indian fast bowler Malcolm Marshall in the Georgetown Test in West Indies in 1983. A vicious short ball from Marshall struck Gavaskar directly on the forehead. The impact was such that the ball bounced right back from Gavaskar's forehead and landed 10–15 feet away. Sunil Gavaskar did not flinch after that spine-chilling hit. He stood his ground, got right behind the line of the next ball and drove it straight past Malcolm

Marshall like a bullet to reach his 50 – a shot that inspired the entire team; a tale of extraordinary courage.

Coach's Corner

Face hostile and unpleasant situations directly. When you get a clear picture of the situation, you can decide the course of action with more clarity – whether to engage or leave alone. In most cases, the issues get mitigated or resolved, because you chose to deal with them directly. If you ignore unpleasant situations, they will grow bigger and come back to haunt you later.

No Ball

Running away from unpleasant situations. Appeasing people. Postponing issues because they are uncomfortable.

Remember the 1989 Tiananmen Square visual? The 'Tank Man'? A lone unarmed figure, holding two shopping bags, stepped in front of a column of armoured tanks as they rolled in to quell civil resistance in the heart of Beijing. Surprised at the man's defiance, the first of the tanks swerved to avoid him. He stepped in front of it again, and again, daring it to crush him as it came within handshaking distance. Defeated, the tank stopped, and with it, all the other tanks behind it as well. The Tank Man climbed onto the first tank, spoke into the gunners hatch and alighted after a short conversation, waving at them to turn back. The tanks restarted and he jumped in front of the tanks again bringing them to a halt. It was not a cricket ball; it was a tank, and he got in line with it. It was so symbolic of the power of human spirit versus machines of war. One act of courage is all it needs to lift all of humanity. You can crush the body, but not the spirit.

It is with the same courage that Sunil Gavaskar, someone who knows what it is to step into the line of hostile enemy fire, single-handedly walked up and saved a Muslim family from being set on fire by a mob during the Mumbai communal riots of 1992-93. "You will have to kill me first," he told the aggressors. The murderous mob walked away in the face of such determined resistance. Courage is just that – to stand up in the line of fire for what one believes in.

In my own experience, being Chief Selector for the Hyderabad Cricket Association required me to face some nasty stuff. Not the straightforward short-pitched stuff that we can handle, but the underhand variety. Threats, accusations, allegations, smear campaigns, conspiracies and all sorts of shenanigans are at play – a regular day at office for cricket selectors I guess. At one point, you do wonder if it's worth it, because you are fast losing friends and making enemies of them. But then you think of those people who trusted you with the job, of setting the right example, of at least one person to whom justice can be done. For me, walking away was the easiest thing to do, but I stayed in line.

Bonus Runs

When you step in line, you learn to handle difficulty, hostility and unpleasantness. Facing these three friends makes you stronger. You will feel free after getting that baggage out of the way. You will have more energy left with you to do creative work.

Exercise: Take a pen and paper. Write down all the areas in your life that you are running away from and pick three of the most important. Get into the line of action. Speak to the person. Do the act. You will be surprised at how easy it is to handle the issue once you get in line with the problem.

---

2 | LOVE

"Faith makes all things possible... love makes all things easy." – Dwight L Moody

It is timing, not power.

THERE ARE TWO WAYS to do things – the hard way and the easy way. This applies to batting as well. Good batsmen do not use the dominant, powerful hand to send the cricket ball flying off the bat to the boundary (not the right hand for right-handers, and vice versa for left-handers) as one would imagine. It is their non-dominant left hand that comes into play and guides the bat, while the right hand supports it. It is the left elbow that rises high to get the bat to follow through in a straight arc and keeps the bat in position to address the ball. It is so, because cricket is about timing, not power. It is about greater results with almost no effort.

In these days of brutal hard-hitting, it is difficult to conceive of aggression of a different variety – the effortless way. Let us visit one of the greatest exhibitions of batsmanship in the Indian sub-continent – the elegant GR Vishwanath decimating a belligerent West Indian attack in Chennai in the 1974-75 Test series between India and the West Indies. Walking in with India placed precariously at 41 for 4, GRV scored an unbeaten 97 in an innings rated by most critics as truly master class, known for its silken counter attacking quality. Spearheaded by the genuinely quick Andy Roberts, the West Indian bowling symbolized brute strength. GRV, standing at 5 feet 2 inches, slender and frail, met that savage power with superbly timed cuts and flicks, and directed the ball to various parts of the ground, all love and timing. India, 55 for 6 at one stage, won the Test match.

In the same breath, watch VVS Laxman, Mohammad. Azharuddin and Saurav Ganguly caress the ball delicately with their bat. Notice how the ball speeds across the grass with minimum effort after it meets the willow. These gentlemen do not bludgeon the ball into submission with needless power. They invite the ball to meet the sweetest part of their bat, making it a willing participant in the process. Only love can make such magic happen. Love is the most powerful weapon after all.

Fielding in the slip cordon for the first time, I grabbed greedily as the ball came flying at me. Not used to such uncultured behaviour, the ball refused my crude advances, shied away and popped out. In time, I learned that the ball, like life itself (or people in general), does not come to you when you grab at it. It comes to you when you have hands that receive it with love.

Coach's Corner

To conquer, you don't need force. To be strong, learn to yield. When you deal from a position of love, you achieve more with less. Love is a creative thought that can change the way you work, live or play. It ensures far greater results with minimum effort.

No Ball

Being rigid and inflexible. Overreacting. Dealing from a space of insecurity. Not looking for better solutions. Jumping to conclusions.

Mahatma Gandhi knew this principle well — it was not about power at all. He achieved more with his non-violent ways than what armies, swords, guns and cannons could have. Be it dealing with the British, the communal riots or the caste-driven segregation of untouchables, he approached each situation with the deadliest weapon of all; love. The Mahatma knew well the power of doing things more efficiently. It was something that all the master timers in the game, the Laxmans, Vishwanaths, also figured out.

Driving in the chaotic traffic of Hyderabad taught me a valuable lesson. In the beginning, my normal reaction to another vehicle moving aggressively into my space was to speed up and secure my position in a game of one-upmanship. But in time, I realized that this competitive reaction makes the other person insecure as well. He speeds up too, causing a deadlock and more needless aggression. On the contrary, when I slowed down, I noticed the other person did the same, and allowed me to go first. It was almost automatic. Was it the uncertainty of the speed or the loss of energy in the situation? I don't know, but by yielding, I realized I get my way easily.

I used the yielding principle in a series of vicious meetings with some aggressive mischief-makers. When I went hard, they came harder at me and nothing got resolved. I remembered the traffic lesson and I let go. Unsure of my position, they vented their grievances. I listened, instead of negating them or forcing them to see my point. That subtle shift in my approach changed everything and they cooled down. I got what I wanted without expending any energy. There is always a way to get more by doing less.

Bonus Runs

When you approach life flexibly like water, you achieve more in the long run with less effort. You are less pressured and more in control. You achieve more with less effort.

Exercise: Pick a situation where you are rigid and unyielding, insecure and not confident. A situation where you are not getting commensurate results for your effort. Step back. Make space for the opposite viewpoint and genuinely consider other perspectives with love. Watch the outcome change when you change your attitude.

---

3 | PATIENCE

"Genius is eternal patience." – Michelangelo

Allow the ball to come to you.

IF YOU THOUGHT BATTING was about going after the ball and knocking the leather off it, think again. Much of batting is about waiting. The best batsmen allow the ball to come to them and only then play it. They do not chase the ball with preconceived notions. Allowing the ball to come to them helps them to play each ball with complete focus and control, play in their area of strength, make fine adjustments and get better timing. Watching the experts bat – from Don Bradman to Sunil Gavaskar and Sachin Tendulkar – helps us understand why they seem to have so much more time. Be it fast bowling or slow bowling, they let the ball come to them first and only then do they address it.

The same patience makes a great finisher like Dhoni wait till the last over of the match before making the final push at the target. Most batsmen cannot handle the pressure of waiting and get out trying too much too soon. But the best in the game wait, outlast the bowler's nerve and patience, allow the moment to build and launch their attack at the right time.

As a young cricketer, I was always in a hurry to hit the ball, seek instant gratification and impress my pals. I'd connect a few shots and then predictably, my innings would end. There was no thinking about lasting longer or fighting it out, just mindless cricket. But there came a day when we were chasing 140 or so in an inter-collegiate match against Jawaharlal Nehru Technological University (JNTU), Hyderabad. We did not have enough batting to finish the job if I got out. I committed myself to eternity. I allowed the ball to come to me, which was a fine way of avoiding the many indiscretions of a batsman. Scoring was difficult, wickets were falling. The opponents, led by my brother Ram, were equal to the task. The contest was even, until one bad ball was bowled and an extra run was conceded. The momentum shifted slightly. The moment had come. I held onto it gratefully and scored off that loose over. I remained unbeaten on 65 and we won the match.

Coach's Corner

Allow life to come to you. If you interfere with the process of life ahead of time, you may complicate issues needlessly and your response will not be the best. If you wait, most issues may get sorted out before they get to you. Let the moment come to you and then engage. The right moment to engage is when you feel your preparation matches the requirement of that moment. Be patient.

No Ball

Jumping ahead of yourself needlessly. Panicking. Feeling an urge to act without being prepared for it.

One of the wisest men I knew, Mr Devidas, once told me his story. As a 14-year-old living with his uncle, he was afflicted with an eye condition that left him practically blind. His cousin, who went to the same school, was his sole connection to a dark world. Tragedy struck when the young cousin passed away due to a sudden illness. Deeply distressed, young Devidas wondered if he should give up on this hazy life, too. His mind was almost made up, but at the last moment he decided to wait. "Let's see what tomorrow brings," he told himself. The next morning, he awoke to a new day… then another, and another. Within a month there was news of a foreign doctor, an eye surgeon, who would be visiting their area. Young Devidas was operated upon and miraculously, he regained 80 percent vision in one eye. A new world opened up – he studied, got a job, married the woman he loved, had two wonderful children, worked at the CIEFL (now EFLU), a stint at the BBC and lived to a ripe old age writing many books in English. "Let's see," he had said to himself and let life come to him before he acted. Things sorted themselves out. Mr Devidas displayed all the qualities of an expert batsman as he waited for the ball to come to him before playing it.

Sitting alongside our boss Mr Kumar, we learned the importance of patience in negotiations. He would sit absolutely still and would say no more than he was required to. Unable to wait, less experienced stakeholders would show their cards one after another. By the time the negotiations came to the business end, Mr Kumar would know the positions and apprehensions of most others. Most times, we'd be surprised how some issues we had perceived as challenges got resolved during the course of the meeting itself. It was his rule – wait and allow things to come to you.

In a key moment in *The Godfather*, an impatient Sonny Corleone blurts out his interest in narcotic trader Solozzo's offer in a meeting presided by the Godfather. That act of impatience encourages Solozzo to attempt to kill Don Corleone, who is opposed to his deal, thereby triggering the saga of revenge that consumes many, including Sonny Corleone and Solozzo among others. If only Sonny had played cricket, he would have allowed the ball to come to him.

Bonus Runs

When you are patient and allow the moment to come to you, the quality of your response is spontaneous and superior. It saves you much trouble and worry.

Exercise: Pick a situation that is worrying you right now. Stop and think: Do you feel like doing something rash, because you cannot deal with the tension of waiting? Do you feel like giving up? Hold yourself. Practice the waiting game – wait for the moment to come to you. You will find that life is easier than you think.

---

4 | AGGRESSION

"In every battle there comes a time when both sides consider themselves beaten, then he who continues the attack wins."
– Ulysses S Grant

Attack. Seize the initiative. Hit the ground running.

TO PLAY COMPETITIVE, entertaining cricket you have to attack. Attacking is being fully prepared, giving your best upfront and seizing the advantage when the moment comes, as opposed to taking time to get into the action. Attacking is not wild, thoughtless, out-of-control action, such as playing reckless shots, bowling bouncers needlessly or sledging. An attacking mindset looks to dominate deliberately and pick holes in the opponent's defences precisely, carefully and patiently. Batsmen look to take singles, rotate strikes and hit the odd boundary. Bowlers create pressure by bowling tight and getting wickets.

Fielders deny runs, push for run outs, pull off catches and build pressure.

Virender Sehwag's 309 in Multan against Pakistan in the 2003-04 Test series between India and Pakistan demonstrates the value of attack. Batting first, India scored 675 in the first innings at a blistering pace propelled by Sehwag's 309 in 375 balls. He put to sword an attack that included Shoaib Akhtar, Mohammed Sami and Saqlain Mushtaq among others. Thanks to that rapid fire innings, India had the luxury of having three days to bowl Pakistan out twice, which they did. It was the first time that India won in 21 years against Pakistan on Pakistan's own soil. Undoubtedly, it was Sehwag's attack that gave India such a huge advantage and made this possible. Now, if anyone thinks that Sehwag's batting is not about precision and preparation, think again; he is one among four batsmen who scored two triple hundreds in Test cricket. Giving him company in his elite club are the likes of Sir Donald Bradman, Brian Lara and Chris Gayle, all attacking batsmen.

Chasing Hyderabad's 325, opponents Tamil Nadu were 180 for 1, well on the way to a first innings lead and with it, the match. We had let the game drift that day and did not give our best. The next day, we regrouped and attacked. We had a two-pronged strategy – stifle the batsmen for runs and prise them out, one by one. Our opponents held onto the advantage they had gained. Over after over, hour after hour, we denied them runs. One wicket, and then another, and another. At the stroke of tea, they were 290 for 4, having managed a mere 110 runs in two sessions. We had slowly but surely gained a slender advantage. Once we broke through the next wicket, their batting collapsed. Venkatapathy Raju got six of the finest in that late evening spell at the KSCA and we won. In our minds, we knew what we were doing – attack all the way.

Coach's Corner

Come prepared and give your best up front at all times. Keep the pressure on from the beginning. Attacking is a proactive mindset. Even in defence, be in an attacking mode. Even in retreat, think of attacking. When you look to act first, you prepare better. Be the one who dictates terms. You will win more often than lose with this approach.

No Ball

Complacency. False modesty. Assumptions. Waiting for approval. Being easily satisfied. Being unprepared. Giving your power away. Following meekly.

In military strategy, offence is the preferred method as it gives the aggressor the advantage of surprising the enemy. While looking up military strategies on the internet, I found 47 attacking strategies as opposed to eight defensive strategies.

One of the greatest battles of all time is the battle at Gaugamela where Alexander the Great defeated Darius III of Persia with an army that was less than half the size of the mighty Persian army. Darius even offered Alexander half of his kingdom to avoid war; an offer that Alexander refused. It is an act that gives an insight into Alexander's attacking mindset. Forced to fight, Darius III entered the war, having all the advantages of battling at home. He chose a wide, open terrain prepared to suit his large army and his scythed chariots, leaving no room for Alexander's armies to hide, and was first at the battleground. But Alexander manoeuvred his smaller armies in a manner that threw the stronger Persian armies into disarray, neutralized their strengths and forced Darius to flee. Alexander attacked deliberately, precisely and seized the initiative as the game changed. This was indeed aggression at its best.

In an important job interview in Mumbai, I chose not to attack upfront when the moment came. I did not put my best foot forward. My entire approach in the group discussion and interview was let-us-see-what-happens, instead of let-me-give-

my-best-shot. The others in the group took the initiative and held onto it, and I let them. By the time I found my rhythm, the interview was over. Little wonder that I did not make it. Today, when I look back, I wonder how I expected to get selected if I was sitting on the back foot instead of attacking. This was just the wrong mindset to take to a competition. As I remember, it is a mindset that I took to my early jobs too, and one that did not serve me well. I learned that there is no point waiting for someone to prod me to give my best; it's better to go prepared and give my best upfront. Attack is the quality of response to the moment when it comes to you; it does not mean rushing in without adequate preparation.

Bonus Runs

Attack is a state that keeps you prepared. It keeps you thinking and improvising. It can fetch you many quick and unexpected gains.

Exercise: Pick any situation where you are unsure of yourself. In all likelihood, it is a situation where you are not fully prepared, that is, mentally you are in a reactive state. Convert those moments by getting into a proactive mindset. Seize control. Seize initiative. You have so much power and freedom. You always have the choice to act first. You have the freedom to set the pace.

---

5 | STRATEGY

"Strengths are not activities you're good at, they're activities that strengthen you. A strength is an activity that before you're doing it you look forward to doing it; while you're doing it, time goes by quickly and you can concentrate; after you've done it, it seems to fulfill a need of yours." – Marcus Buckingham

Play to your strengths.

TO STRATEGIZE FOR GAINING a competitive advantage, one must be aware of one's strengths and weaknesses and what to do with them. Most of us are caught in a dilemma of whether we should work on our weaknesses or play to our strengths. As a basic strategy, successful cricketers play to their strengths and do not worry too much about their weaknesses. They know that one well-honed strength gives them a clear, competitive edge to beat the rest. Since strengths provide the leverage to propel them farthest, they work on honing them. Working excessively on weaknesses does not provide any specific advantage and might compromise strengths. When blessed with an advantage, use it.

The documentary film *Fire in Babylon* analyzes how the West Indian team shed the demeaning tag of merely being entertaining Calypso cricketers, who did not mind losing to ruthless world beaters. Going in to play with no strategy except to be happy-go-lucky entertainers, the West Indies team lost 5–1 to a relentless Australia. Having learned their lesson the hard way the West Indies team, led by captain Clive Lloyd, went back to the strategy room. They identified their fastest bowlers, trained them and unleashed them with a clear intent to gain a strategic advantage. Silent, quick, lethal and terrifying, the Windies quicks comprising of Andy Roberts, Michael Holding, Wayne Daniel, Colin Croft, Joel Garner, Sylvester Clarke and Malcolm Marshall struck terror into the hearts of their opponents even before the beginning of the match. So fearsome was the exhibition of pace and power by the West Indies on the English tour of 1976, that it was considered dangerous to the game. The West Indies dominated world cricket for the next 20 years with this strategy.

At about the same time in the 1970s, the Indian team used four spinners in tandem. Young Indian skipper

Mansur Ali Khan Pataudi was quick to realize his team's unique strengths and used Bishen Singh Bedi, Errapalli Prasanna, BS Chandrasekhar and Venkatraghavan to his advantage. After an over or two by a makeshift medium pacer to take the shine off the ball, the Indian spinners would be in business, eaving their magic around visiting sides that floundered against their subtle variations. The quartet played 231 tests between them, got 853 wickets and starred in Test victories against West Indies, England, Australia and New Zealand.

The star studded Tamil Nadu juniors side with the likes of L Sivaramakrishnan, WV Raman and B Arun, all of whom went on to play for India, was coasting along towards the first innings lead. The above mentioned heavies, of whom LS had already represented India, were to bat next. Our stand-in skipper Vivek Jaisimha backed my strength to use the old ball well and get it to seam a bit. He used me in a long spell after lunch at one end (instead of using a spinner as was conventionally done). I got enough assistance from the old ball to send back all three batsmen in one spell and we contained the Tamil Nadu side to a reasonable total.

Coach's Corner

Identify your strengths and play to them. It is your easiest route to success. When you put your energies behind your strengths, you leverage maximum advantage for yourself. Work 80% on honing your strengths and 20% on improving your weaknesses. As your strengths grow, your weaknesses will naturally diminish.

No Ball

False modesty. Not knowing your strengths and believing that you have none. Losing attitude. Worrying excessively about weaknesses.

Superstar Amitabh Bachchan struggled before he made a mark in the Hindi film industry. Film producers felt he looked unconventional and was too tall. His famous voice was rejected by the AIR twice. But Amitabh Bachchan persisted, knowing that it is not about weaknesses, it is what you do with your strengths that matters. Among his perceived weaknesses, he found many strengths, too – his talent, hunger and his work ethic. Not surprisingly, his weaknesses turned out to be his strengths in time.

Having no strategy for campus interviews after college cost me dearly. For the first few interviews, I even hid my strengths and played on my weak areas. Instead of projecting my unique strengths of having been a first class cricketer, a University captain, a committed team player, a good communicator, a decent personality – all of which could have been presented well to gain an advantage, I played on areas that others were better at, academic scores, for example. Funnily, for a long time, I never even saw my strengths as my strengths and perhaps, even saw them as weaknesses. Now, you cannot help a person who sees his strengths as his weaknesses can you? It took a while for me to understand that there are no prizes for being excessively modest. Or stupid.

Bonus Runs

When you focus on your strengths, you use yourself better. You do what you do well naturally and worry less about what you cannot do. Better results follow.

Exercise: Make a list of your strengths. If you don't know them (most of us don't), ask those who know you. How many of your strengths are you using to get what you want? Rate their usage on a scale of 1 to 10. If you are not using them fully, use them more. Work on them to make them stronger. Keep track of your results. You will be a completely different proposition now.

---

6 | DILIGENCE

"Diligence is the mother of good luck." – Benjamin Franklin

Keep your head down. Take it session by session.

WHEN INDIA WON THE WORLD CUP in 1983, the odds were 1 to 66 against India winning. Obviously, no one was really thinking much about India winning the Cup. Kapil Dev's team did not complicate the issue by thinking too far ahead. It kept its head down and progressed, match by match. The team scraped past Zimbabwe in the league, beat England in the semis and pipped the formidable West Indies in the final to win the Cup. In the 2011 World Cup, India threw off a sluggish start, outlasted a combative Australia in the quarter finals, an unpredictable Pakistan in the semifinals and a canny Sri Lanka in the finals. Addressing the job at hand with total concentration ensures steady and safe progress and is a good recipe for success. Cricketers train to break their jobs down match by match, session by session and under stress, even ball by ball.

Keeping the head down is an important aspect of cricketing technique, both figuratively and literally. By keeping the head down, the batsman concentrates on the point of contact with the ball, the defining moment in the act, and is not enamoured with the ensuing result. When batsmen play shots with their head in the air, they fail to connect and stand a good chance of getting out. Watch any big hitting batsman like MS Dhoni, Yuvraj Singh, Virat Kohli, Chris Gayle or Glen Maxwell hit a six and watch their head and their eyes at the point of contact. The head is down and the eyes are focused on the job at hand.

For ten years, the Osmania University team did not win the South Zone Championships. For five of those years, I was part of strong teams that lost to far weaker teams. I knew that we lost, because we did not keep our head down. We didn't take it match by match. We were already looking at the final, instead of playing the current match – the equivalent of looking at the boundary line instead of the ball while hitting it. In 1991, my last year at the university, I wanted to set the record straight. While strategizing about how to approach the tournament, I expressed my view to my captain, my good friend Vijay Kumar, that we should keep our head down and take it match by match. We beat Calicut University, scraped past a tough

Bangalore University in the semis and beat Madras University in the final to achieve our dream after a decade. There remains no doubt in my mind that our team won because we did not get ahead of ourselves enamoured by future glory.

Coach's Corner

To rise high, keep your head down. Take one measured step at a time. Ensure that your present job is done well, detail by detail, meticulously. Keeping the head down is the difference between hoping and ensuring that you get what you want. In situations that overwhelm you, make it simple take – things one at a time, one day at a time. A little progress a day is all you need to walk 10,000 miles.

No ball

Overconfidence. Being overwhelmed by difficulty. Looking beyond the current moment. Worrying about the past. Careless work. Not putting the required effort.

Mountain climbers prepare for years to summit Mount Everest. They do not dash up to the summit carelessly, nor do they collapse in a heap and give up on encountering any difficulties. They take one careful step at a time. One slip and they know it's back to the pavilion.

New Zealander Mark Englis, the first double amputee to scale Mount Everest on prosthetic legs, writes in his book *Legs on Everest* about the physical and mental preparation that goes into climbing Everest. One needs to build the strength and stamina to last the challenge, and resistance to the altitude, cold and illness; one needs to cultivate a diligent mindset. The prospect of injury and death is real and immediate and makes climbers extremely cautious and careful. Englis summitted the Everest on May 15, 2006 along with the HIMEX expedition of 2006 led by Russel Brice – an expedition that consisted of four guides, 11 climbers, 16 members of a camera crew, ten sherpas and six cooks. The climbers, he mentions, are more careful during the descent, which is considered more treacherous than the climb. One cannot ever think beyond the current step. Despite all the preparation and planning, Englis suffered serious injuries to both his leg stumps during the descent and his fingers sustained frost bite.

As a rookie writer, I'd find nothing more irritating than readers who comment on spelling mistakes and punctuation and not on the story. Why are they so bothered about the small details, I'd think? But after reading other amateur works, I realized that the big picture is lost if one does not take care of the small details. In fact, the big picture looks beautiful when the small details are handled well. By taking care of those minor irritants, the reader can then focus on the big story.

Bonus Runs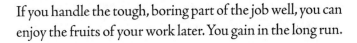

If you handle the tough, boring part of the job well, you can enjoy the fruits of your work later. You gain in the long run.

Exercise: Write down your big goals. Break them into large chunks. Break down the first chunk into smaller parts until you have broken it down enough to get started on it. The key is to start working on it day by day, hour by hour. Once you start, keep going, taking one step at a time. Put all your focus into each step and do it well. You will end up doing a fine job in the end.

---

7 | SIMPLIFY

"Our life is frittered away by detail… simplify, simplify."
– Henry David Thoreau

Keep It Simple.

IT IS ONE OF MS DHONI'S PET THEORIES to keep things simple, but obviously, keeping things simple is not simple. To eliminate non-essentials and focus on essentials requires great clarity. To see the obvious requires the vision of a simpleton. Observe Glen McGrath or Anil Kumble bowl and you find that much of their success is owed to keeping it simple. There is nothing extravagant or complex about their procedure – nagging accuracy, engaging the batsmen constantly and making them play at deliveries, – just enough to send the batsman back. Similarly, great batsmen make batting look uncomplicated as they focus on putting bat to ball.

The strong Andhra Bank team had lost half their side. I ran in to bowl to Khursheed, who had just arrived at the crease at no. 7. After a couple of balls, our skipper ML Jaisimha sauntered up to me from mid off. "Harry," he asked in that deep baritone voice of his, "do you remember how you got him last year?" Yes, I bowled a short ball at him and he fended it to the gully. "Then what are you waiting for?" he asked simply. What? Was it so simple? Perhaps, I had been lucky last time? Anyway, I bounced the next ball. Khursheed fended it to the gully, where Vidyuth took the catch in an exact repeat of last year. "See," said he. It opened my eyes to how we complicate our lives by second-guessing everything. I used the same philosophy with good success many times later and it worked every time.

Chasing a total of 420 set by Nizam College against our Osmania University Campus Colleges team, we were staring down the barrel of the gun at 180 for 8. I joined my senior from engineering college, Ajay, in the middle. Having no clue as to what to do, we decided to keep it simple. Just survive, we told one another. We kept it simple and addressed each ball as it came. So engrossed were we in surviving, that we did not realize we had put up a 180-run partnership, that our team total had reached 408, that I had got a 100 and Ajay a 50. I can think of several such performances that resulted when we kept it simple. Unfortunately, we complicate things too much, too often and consequently, underperform.

Coach's Corner

Simplify to the bare essentials. Keep all jobs simple. When you keep it simple, you get the results you want. Address the issue directly. Say it like it is. See it like it is. Deal with it. Life is simple.

No Ball

Too much thinking. Second-guessing yourself. Not being in the moment. Beating around the bush. Missing the obvious. Not wanting to see a changed reality.

The purpose of a business is to satisfy the customer's need, a school to educate, a hospital to heal, a government to govern. But we forget to keep it simple and complicate things. Businesses forget their customers, indulge themselves in building financial ratios and valuations and forget their core reason to be in the business. Schools forget about teaching and aiding in the wholesome growth of students and worry about rankings. Hospitals concentrate on turnovers and profits, and would rather keep the patient sick than heal them. Governments worry about staying in power through populist means, forgetting the good of the people who elected them. If we simplify, everything falls into place. If businesses took care of their customers, hospitals their patients, schools their students and governments their people, they would not have to worry about being wanted and staying relevant.

One of my favourite stories is 'The Emperor's New Clothes' a short tale by Hans Christian Anderson that appears in the collection *Fairy Tales Told for Children*. The story of the foolish emperor who loves exotic new clothes is an apt example to showcase how simple issues can be complicated to ridiculous levels. Knowing of the emperor's weakness for new clothes, two strangers promise him a magical suit, one so extraordinary that it would not be visible to those who are unfit, incompetent or stupid. They charge a lot of gold for their magical suit, banking on human tendency to complicate things and not simply see them as they are. After a few days, the two cheats emerge from their room and mime the act of putting on a fine suit upon the emperor. The emperor cannot see the suit, but he does not want to be seen as unfit, incompetent or stupid and keeps silent. All the subjects who see their emperor wearing no clothes stay silent too, because they do not wish to be seen as incompetent, unfit or stupid. Finally, a small boy cries out loudly that the emperor is wearing no clothes and brings the story to an end. Don't we see that happening often even today?

While doing the vipassana course, I heard this story. The master saw a man sweating profusely while practicing the meditation technique. His shirt was drenched in sweat and his face contorted. When the master enquired if he was feeling any sensation, he shook his head. No, he replied agitatedly. Try as he might, he was not feeling any sensation, he complained. The master pointed out to him that since he was looking for divine sensations, he seemed to be ignoring a gross sensation like pain. That is how we complicate our lives and not see what is staring us in the face. If he had kept it simple, he would have surely noticed the intense pain. But he was worried about the divine sensations that others were feeling while he was not.

Bonus Runs

When you keep it simple, it gives you one target to work at with complete concentration. You go with the flow. Results improve.

Exercise: Pick a situation that is appearing complex to you now. Strip it to the essentials — the what, where, why, how and when of it. See it like it is. Address the issue as it is. You will find it far more bearable.

---

8 | PERSEVERANCE

"Success is the child of drudgery and perseverance. It cannot be coaxed or bribed; pay the price and it is yours."
– Orison Swett Marden

The match is not over till the last ball is bowled.

MANY OF US GIVE UP when the tide turns against us. We do not invest any further effort for a seemingly lost cause and start to look for reasons to blame. The issue is lost in the mind even before it is actually lost in reality. However, cricketers are told time and again that games can change suddenly and that they must persevere till the last ball is bowled. More often than not, this perseverance creates a window of opportunity and turns the match on its head. It's not luck that changes the game. It's the choice one makes between giving up and persevering. It is fuelled by the quality of that perseverance; an underlying desire to win.

The history of cricket throws up many last ball victories and dramatic collapses. Javed Miandad's improbable six off Chetan Sharma's last delivery at Sharjah in the dramatic final of Austral-Asia Cup on April 18, 1986, changed the texture of the game in one ball and had an impact on Indian cricket that went far beyond that game. Batting first, India piled on 245 in its allotted 50 overs with contributions from centurion Sunil Gavaskar and half centuries from K Srikkanth and Dilip Vengsarkar. In reply, old rival Pakistan was staring down the barrel at 241 for 9 with the last recognized batsman Javed Miandad holding one end and the number 11 batsman at the other. Needing four runs to win off the last ball, the combative Miandad hit Chetan Sharma's full toss for a six and secured a highly unlikely win for Pakistan. If there's one thing that cricket teaches you, it's that it's never over till it's over.

The final of a private tournament in the Old City of Hyderabad. A super charged atmosphere. We, the outsiders, were playing the local team, the favourites. Batting first, we were shot out for a mere 72, but we did not give up. We wanted to win badly. The opponents struggled as we defended our meager total with every ounce of strength we had. By the end of the 22ⁿᵈ over, our opponents were 71 for 4. With a mere two runs to win, five wickets in hand and plenty of overs to go, one would say there was no hope for us. In that dark situation, our optimistic captain Imtiaz, a non-regular bowler, decided to bowl himself. In one miraculous first over, he got four wickets and reduced the opposition to 71 for 8 (which in effect was nine wickets down as one batsman was injured). My wily chum Timothy Paul got the last man caught behind from the other end. We won the match by one run. If you ask me today, I'd say with certainty that we did not win by luck, we fought like tigers through every ball of their innings and created that magic moment. I know, because I put in every ounce of effort into my five overs where I got the first four batsmen and injured the other. It was that persevering effort that saw us through, not luck. You see, in cricket, you never know until the last ball is bowled.

Coach's Corner

Never give up. Keep at it till the very end. Even the most hopeless of situations can change in a moment. What's the hurry to lose? To give up? Focus on effort. Miracles happen if you hang in there. Keep the effort going with the same intensity.

No ball

Useless, defeatist thoughts. Giving up before it's over. Not putting in the effort. Defusing pressure by taking the foot off the accelerator in the end.

In the classic book *Think and Grow Rich*, author Napolean Hill tells a story that highlights the value of perseverance. It was gold rush time and a man found a vein of ore. He raised money, bought machinery and began digging. He found gold and repaid all his debts. But soon after, the vein disappeared. He kept digging and found nothing. Frustrated, he gave up, sold the machinery to a junk dealer and quit. The junk dealer, however, was a man who seemed to know his cricket. He hired a mining engineer, who checked the mine and calculated that there was a vein of gold a mere three feet from where the previous owner had stopped digging. The junk man made millions from the mine. Persevere and you could be one ball away, three feet away, from a change in fortune.

Desperately short of targets by a massive 20 million on the last day of the public issue, our sales team was dejected. All avenues had been exhausted. We had tapped every nook and corner of the state, every single agent and associate, visited every single prospect, contacted high net worth clients and left no stone unturned in a massive effort. There seemed to be nothing else to do. But Kumar, our indefatigable boss wouldn't throw in the towel. With only a couple of hours to go, he made us call all our prospects again. It seemed like a pointless exercise by this time, and on a Saturday, too! But miraculously, at noon, in one public sector company that had shut down several years ago, a company that did not work weekends, someone answered the phone. The man had 30 million from the company's PF Trust to invest. We threw everything aside and raced to his office. That experience reinforced all that I learned on the cricket field; it's important to focus on the effort and play the game till the very end. You never know how it will change. You get help from the most unexpected quarters.

Bonus Runs

When you hang in there till the end, you will find more miracles coming your way. You end up on the winning side more often than not.

Exercise: List all the times when you had mentally given up before you exhausted all avenues open to you. Now train yourself to hold your space with a neutral thought. What situation in the present makes you feel like giving up? Keep the effort going even if it appears pointless. Keep track of the results with this neutral approach.

---

9 | EFFORT

"Continuous effort – not strength or intelligence – is the key to unlocking your potential." – Winston Churchill

Bend Your Back.

IN CRICKET, "BEND YOUR BACK" is a phrase that teammates normally use to prod fast bowlers into putting in that little extra effort into their bowling. It is a literal term, because fast bowlers tend to get stiff and lazy and sometimes do not bend their back while completing their action. Not bending their back compromises pace, swing and seam, making them less effective. When in full flow, fast bowlers are a totally different proposition to batsmen – from pace to nip, control to swing, cut to seam – everything starts working once they bend their back. Similarly, batsmen lean into their shots, go low and get their head over the ball, an act that requires extra effort to get a better result. Fielders "get down to the ball" by keeping their body weight low and almost hug the ground to be ready to stop or catch the ball safely. When they make lazy and halfhearted efforts without bending down, the ball goes between their legs and runs are lost. Bending the back is about giving that little extra effort each time.

Big hitting Sandeep Patil was getting the measure of our bowling in the end overs of an Arlem Trophy game. I found good rhythm and backed myself to bowl some effort balls, when he hit me for a massive six over long on. So loud, so hard was it hit that I can still hear the sound of his bat ringing in my ears to this day. I was stunned at the ferocity of that assault. "It's okay Harry boy, bend your back," came the call from my captain Ehtesham from behind the stumps. Reassured, I bowled the next ball with even more effort. That ball got some extra bounce and took the thick edge of Sandeep Patil's bat on the way to the keeper. Bending my back paid off and I got a prize wicket.

Coach's Corner

Effort is an absolute must if you wish to succeed at anything. That little extra effort you put into your work is what makes the big difference in the end. It's like adding a cherry to the top of the ice cream. Giving your best effort, and then some more effort, is the way forward to the next level.

No Ball

Slacking off. Making halfhearted attempts. Hoping. Believing in luck. Blame. Criticism.

In the book *Mindset – The Psychology of Winning*, author Carol Dwycke, explains how growth-oriented people believe in effort and how in a fixed mindset, people believe only in abstract stuff (like talent, which does not help once the standard of the field increases beyond a point). Those who believe in effort and growth keep improving all their life. The ones who do not believe in effort tend to blame, lie, make excuses and over time, fall to seed. Michael Jordan, Tiger Woods, Rafael Nadal and every champion in their league have proven this. Champions work harder than anyone else.

Similarly, in the recent election campaign for the 2014 elections, one could see the effort put in by Prime Minister Narendra Modi. He really bent his back addressing over 440 rallies during his grueling campaign, not taking any chances. An effort that paid off big time for him as the election results showed – a thumping majority in the Parliament for his party the Bharatiya Janata Party.

I'd asked the MBA students of my Entrepreneurship Development course from the University of Hyderabad, to make a presentation of their business plans. I was amazed to see the effort one of the students put into his presentation. Despite not being very fluent in the language and not used to public speaking, Shravan Kumar hardly skipped a beat. So well was he prepared, so thorough with his numbers, so fluent with his answers, that he received a standing ovation from his peers. Two of the star students bungled terribly with badly prepared presentations, gave excuses and flopped, one abstained and another did a passable presentation. When the group of mock angel investors from his class were asked who they would invest their monies with, Shravan got everyone's money and confidence, and raised 500 percent of what he needed. His effort made up for everything – 'this guy can bend his back' was the message everyone got. Young Shravan can do whatever he sets his mind on now. He has seen the results that bending his back can bring.

Bonus Runs

The extra effort you put in makes all the difference. Give it all you have. Push it.

Exercise: Pick a job at hand. Give your best effort to it. Then push a little more at the end. Long hours, sleepless nights, whatever it takes. See the difference in the output when you give that little extra to every effort. You will see the most unlikely results.

10 | BASICS

"You can't invent Google, Facebook or the iPod unless you've mastered the basics, are willing to put in long hours and can pick yourself up from the floor when life knocks you down the first 10 times." – Amy Chua, Author

Know your basics well.

CHAMPIONS KNOW THEIR BASICS WELL. They make less mistakes than their opponents and self-correct faster. Even when smaller teams upset bigger units, it always comes down to who has done the basics right. Whether it is Kenya beating the West Indies in the 1996 World Cup, Bangladesh beating Pakistan in the 1999 World Cup or Ireland beating England in the 2011 World Cup, the story is always the same. The bowlers bowl in right spots, catches are taken, runs maximized, teammates backed one another, and voila, they pipped the bigger opponents over the line. When such upsets occur, it is time for the losing team to go back to basics.

Bowlers work on the basics of getting their rhythm, accuracy, line and length and their stock ball right. Batsmen work on defensive play and shots they are best at. Fielders secure catching and fielding basics. Successful teams cover basics thoroughly – being fit, fielding well, working on disciplined batting and bowling performances. No wonder then, that the stock reply of most players on their best performances is this – I focused on the basics. Are you doing the basics right?

Chasing 271 against South Africa, Australia was struggling at 120 for 5. Australian skipper Steve Waugh was at the crease, the last hope for Australia to win that game and make it to the World Cup semifinal. When Waugh was on 56 and Australia was 153, he tapped the simplest of catches to Herschelle Gibbs, one of South Africa's best fielders. Gibbs took the catch and tried to flick it in the air before finishing the catch – a basic error. The ball slipped and fell. Waugh scored an unbeaten 120 and took Australia home. South Africa lost a great opportunity to go through to the semifinal. A case of how much harm is done when the basics are ignored.

Coach's Corner

If you want to grow, get your basics right. They provide the foundation and framework on which you can build expertise over time. Practicing and brushing up on basics is time well spent. Your confidence grows. You can challenge the best. When in trouble, go back to the basics. They will save you.

No Ball

Big plans without basics. Inconsistent plans. Shallow and brittle foundations.

Long-lasting brands, strong institutions and reputed companies last longer, because their fundamentals are strong. Companies like Tata Steel, Dabur, Godrej & Boyce and ITC are among the few 100-year-old organizations in India that are still going strong. They keep their focus on the basics – the customer, the stakeholders and the value they deliver. These companies evolve as customer preferences change and keep stakeholder interests paramount. On the other hand, there are several companies that have lost sight of the basics – neglected their customer, stopped creating value and took their stakeholders for granted. We all know the disastrous results that ensued.

While working in the marketing division of my bank as a trainee, I naively assumed that since I was in the marketing division selling the bank's financial products, I could concentrate on the marketing aspects and do without a sound knowledge of the basics of finance. But I realized soon that my perfunctory knowledge in finance would not fool anyone, certainly not the senior executives of prospective clients. I studied the basics of finance again and learned them all thoroughly. Armed with this vital input, I was able to present our products in a customer-centric manner. That helped me immensely in my effort. It also gave me a lot of confidence, which was something that I lacked earlier.

Bonus Runs

Basics guarantee a minimum competence on which you can expand. If you know your basics well, you can aspire for expertise.

Exercise: What are the basics of the activity you wish to pursue? Write them down. If ever you are struggling, spend time and strengthen the same. It is never too late. Else, you will always find it tough to cope. You will be far more confident once the basics are strong.

---

11 | HONESTY

"Almost any difficulty will move in the face of honesty. When I am honest I never feel stupid. And when I am honest I am automatically humble." – Hugh Prather

Play with a straight bat.

FOR THE UNINITIATED, the straight bat is the one that comes straight down from the batsman's back lift in a perpendicular arc to meet the ball. It is a transparent, honest piece of work, eager to do its job with no deceit or shortcut. The straight bat is a prerequisite for any batsman worth his salt. By showing the full face of the bat to the ball, batsmen increase chances of contact and ensure greater safety. It is a finely honed skill and requires practice, concentration, patience and belief in the process. The straight bat respects the ball, the bowler and the game. Batsmen are often known by the pedigree of their straightness as 'straight bats' or 'cross bats'.

On the field, one can easily distinguish between straight bats and cross bats. The straight bats are serene, secure and compact. They display good judgment, balance and confidence. They know the process, have practiced it, are in for the long term and are, therefore, more productive. The cross bats are instable, insecure, impatient and are unwilling to last it out. They do not know the process, are prone to take imprudent risks, look for short-term gratification and are, therefore, less productive. The straight bats are pleasing to watch. The cross bats are not.

Bowling to the straight bats is an education. I remember bowling to Sanjay Manjrekar at his peak and to a very young VVS Laxman when he was still at school level – and they can drive you nuts – their bats appeared as broad as the Great Wall of China. It's difficult as hell to dislodge straight bats.

Coach's Corner

The straight bat follows the path of honesty, hard work and patience. It is upright with no hidden agenda and is willing to work for its reward. To walk the straight path, requires sound values, commitment and a strong character. If you pick the right practices to follow and get your first principles right, it pays off in the long run.

No ball

Dishonesty. Shortcuts. Blaming others. Excuses. Cheating. Flashy behaviour.

We have had several straight bats in our world, who have inspired generations with their outstanding technique. Mahatma Gandhi, Nelson Mandela, Martin Luther King, Jr. are some of the names that come to mind. They were honest, forthright, unwavering and looked after the greater good. Where are such straight bats in society today? We see many more cross bats making their way to the wicket these days – dishonest, short-sighted, fickle and selfish. We need good players who can be role models for generations to come and we certainly need coaches who can teach us the virtues of playing straight. Are you practicing playing with the straight bat?

In 2009, Santiago Gori, a taxi driver in Argentina, returned a bag carrying USD 32,500 that he found in the back seat of his taxi to the rightful owners, an elderly couple. His act of honesty sparked a series of acts of gratitude from Argentines who found this story extraordinary – someone started a website to raise money for him, another promised a GPS for his car, snowboarding lessons, recording a song – among many other things. Santiago, however, was amused, because for him playing with a straight bat was normal.

Working in the bank, I saw both types around me. The ones who invested in right practices earned fame, position, wealth and respect. The ones who were dishonest and corrupt went behind bars and lost their jobs. We face the same choices that any batsman does.

I was clear about my principles and worked honestly in a bank where multi-crore deals were the order of the day. In an entire decade of working at the bank, only one client had the temerity to approach me with a crooked delivery. Having tried to influence me one way or another, through friends and bosses and other means, he resorted to a desperate tactic to get me to present his hopeless case in a better light. The client delivered a mobile phone (new toys those days) home without my knowledge. Thankfully, my mother informed me about it immediately. When I called him and asked him what he was up to, he said he knew my mother was ill and it could be useful. I gave him 15 minutes to get his 'gift' out of my place. He got it out in ten. He never took that route with me after that, nor did anyone else.

Bonus Runs

The right practices help in all formats and bring great

rewards in the long term. You feel empowered to handle all situations.

Exercise: What are the areas in your life where you feel vague, compromised and unsettled? Do some straight and honest thinking. Choose transparency, honesty and integrity in each of these areas. Give up, let go. Do the right thing.

---

12 | MEDITATION

"At the end of the day, I can end up just totally wacky, because I've made mountains of molehills. With meditation, I can keep them as molehills." – Ringo Starr

Play each ball on its merit. Play the ball, not the bowler.

TO FACE EACH MOMENT ANEW is to die every moment and be reborn again. This is the state of mind expected of good batsmen. Playing each ball on its merit is a mantra that batsmen imbibe early. It's not easy unless you've had the training of a monk. To blank out a terrifying ball that almost got you out, injured you, to control the urge to lash out at the next delivery or to forget the reputation of the bowler is difficult. But good batsmen train their minds to get over the demons of the past and the temptations of the future quickly. They live in the present, in the here and now, addressing each ball as it comes in its true form, and by doing so, affect the quality of that relationship. It's a meditative state. It's how the game is played.

In a practice game in Peshawar in 1989, Sachin Tendulkar, all of 16 and on his first tour, hit veteran leg spinner Abdul Qadir for 27 runs in one over, including four sixes. Lesser batsmen would have played Qadir the magician and got themselves out. One can surmise safely that Sachin played the ball instead of the reputation of the bowler.

In his book, *The Art of Captaincy*, former England captain Mike Brearley cites the example of the doughty English batsman John Edrich, who scored 310 runs at Headingley on a seaming wicket against New Zealand. Edrich, beaten at least once every over throughout his innings, came back strongly each time and, on most occasions, scored a boundary off the next ball. A true monk.

One regret I have is not cultivating the stout heart that Edrich and his ilk displayed. Dropped from the Hyderabad Ranji squad as a 20-year-old fast bowler, I meekly accepted that verdict. I chose to remain in the past, and became one of the many 'also played' cricketers. If only I had realized that each day is a new delivery, I could have worked harder, improved and become 'undroppable', instead of giving up after one bad ball. That's a big lesson I learned that I now apply to life, my writing. Each day is a new delivery and I approach it on its merit.

Coach's Corner

Deal with each situation anew. Deal with it on its merit. Engage with facts. Each moment is new and comes with a fresh perspective. Practice this behaviour. It will change the quality of your relationships and many other important aspects of your life.

No ball

Colouring situations with interpretations, opinions and judgments of the past and the future. Missing the present. Overreacting. Inaction.

Abraham Lincoln, one of America's greatest presidents, faced a torrid time from a bowler called Life. Growing up in poverty, failing at business, suffering a nervous breakdown and losing elections for the Congress, Senate and the vice presidential office, did not deter him from becoming the 16th President of the USA. More importantly, Abraham Lincoln did not let his past failures cloud his judgment. He led America admirably through its toughest moral, economic and military crises – the Civil War, abolition of slavery and a weak economy. The astute way in which he engineered the Emancipation Proclamation that led to abolition of slavery against tough opposition is captured brilliantly in the movie *Lincoln* (2012). Abraham Lincoln played each complex delivery on its merit like a master batsman.

In one of the greatest sporting upsets of all time, the US Ice hockey team of 1980 beat a strong USSR team in what is famously known as 'The Miracle on Ice'. The USSR had won six of the past seven Olympic gold medals prior to that game, and led the US 28–7 head to head. The young US team with an average age of 21 years, comprising of collegiate and amateur players, played the puck, not the opponent's reputation, and emerged victorious. From that moment of the 1980 Winter Olympics at Lake Placid, New York has been defined as the 'Top Sport Moment' by *Sports Illustrated* and has inspired a famous movie *Miracle* (2004).

Bonus Runs

An unbiased, non-judgmental and uncluttered approach improves response and judgment. Inter-personal skills and handling of situations improve tremendously. It works wonders in stressful situations.

Exercise 1: List your failures and setbacks. Write down what you learned from them. Making mistakes is fine. Repeating mistakes is not.

Exercise 2: Pick any situation that is bothering you now. Make two columns – in one column write your interpretations of the situation and in the other column write the facts as they are. Drop all interpretations, judgments and opinions on people and situations. Deal only with the facts. Does it take the stress out of the situation? Does it help bring a whole new creative energy into the situation? Analyze.

13 | STILLNESS

"To the mind that is still, the whole universe surrenders."
– Lieh Tzu

"It's what I learn from the great actors that I work with. Stillness. That's all and that's the hardest thing." – Morgan Freeman

Keep your head still.

IN COACHING PARLANCE, the eyes are the camera. Any shake of the head disturbs clarity and affects the outcome. The result of an unsteady head on the cricket field is a missed catch, a misdirected delivery or a missed ball. For best results, batsmen keep their head still while preparing to face the bowler. The bowler's head is still while delivering the ball. The fielder's head is still while preparing to receive the ball. The still head improves concentration, awareness and the quality of your response. Watch Sachin

Tendulkar, Zaheer Khan and Rahul Dravid in action and you'll observe what a still head is all about.

Facing a speedy Robin Singh in my debut Buchi Babu game, on a matting wicket at Marina grounds in Madras, was an experience I cannot easily forget. The first delivery whizzed past me, the second thudded into my thigh, and the third zipped by before I could react. I quickly realized that I needed to do better to avoid collateral damage. The danger of the moment made me go still, and sharpened all my senses as I geared up to face the next ball. I brought my bat to the ball this time and saved myself another bruise. Later that year, I faced another young fast bowler who played for India, Raju Kulkarni, who was quicker than Robin. Better prepared this time, I got a boundary off the only ball I faced; a flick to mid-wicket. Ah, the virtues of a still head.

A place on the cricket field where the still head comes in most handy is while fielding at slips. Any shake of the head and the catch is grassed. The mantra is this – stay still, stay low, keep your eyes on the ball, let it come to you and accept it. No jerks, no grabs. Be still. Easy does it.

Coach's Corner

Stillness heightens concentration, sharpens clarity and deepens the experience. Perfect stillness is 100%

awareness. It keeps your mind balanced on a razor's edge. Because stillness keeps you completely aware, in the perfect now, your response is best.

No Ball

Low focus. A twitching body. Oscillating thoughts.

Watching Buddhist monks meditate is a lesson in stillness. Serene and at peace, in total harmony with the environment around them, they are a picture of perfect stillness. Yet, in that absolute stillness, they appear fully aware, more responsive and clearheaded than the many nervous twitchers around. Watch a big cat as it stalks its prey, a snake as it faces a mongoose, and you know how deadly stillness can be.

Or you could watch Bruce Lee, the legendary martial arts exponent, in action for a lesson in stillness. His body is all coiled up and yet fully relaxed. Watch the precision, the speed and deliberation behind each act in the movie *Enter the Dragon* (1973) as he fights O' Hara and later, the iron-claw wearing villain Han in the *Hall of Mirrors*. John Soet, who worked with Bruce Lee, confirms in an interview that Bruce Lee was so fast that he was just a blur on the camera. They had to slow him down. "The 35mm shutter speeds aren't that fast," Soet said. Such is the stuff that springs from stillness.

I am intrigued by and am constantly in search of that stillness. Such stillness, or the 'gap' as they say, has appeared in rare moments for me, almost by accident. Perhaps in a still moment, a creative idea has slipped in. I may see a path, a goal or a vision in that stillness. I may feel pure emotion and connectedness to something that is also borne out of such stillness.

My best work certainly comes out of stillness. In those moments, I have to pull myself together, not let any thought stray and focus on creating that stillness. Out of that space arises my response. I felt this stillness when I was in the zone while batting or bowling. You can see the act unfolding in a most surreal manner, deliberate and under perfect control. It is almost as if you can will things to happen the way you want them to. While writing, I still myself when I am not able to get my mind around an elusive thought. I can see the difference stillness makes to the quality of thought. Similarly, I try to ensure that stillness in all things that mean much to me, when I need all of myself to be completely involved in the job. I pull myself together and try to just be that act. Then, it unlocks and flows.

Bonus Runs

Stillness helps you to see things clearly. It helps you to act proactively from a space of high awareness. It promotes decisive action.

Exercise: Sit still for as long as you can. No twitching. No thinking. A mind that is not still will not lend itself easily to a still body. Practice being still. Imbibe the essence of that quality. Practice stillness in all things. It helps to see things clearly. When you need to think clearly, close your eyes and find that stillness. The stillness will provide you with the answers.

14 | CONCENTRATION

"Concentration is a fine antidote to anxiety." – Jack Nicklaus

Keep your eyes on the ball always.

IT MAY SEEM LIKE an obvious and elementary detail that cricketers must be told to always keep their eyes on the ball, but it is not easy. Practiced right, keeping your eyes on the ball requires tremendous concentration that drains you mentally. Good batsmen watch the ball coming out of the bowler's hand, even seeing the stitches on the seam and the direction the ball is rotating, till it hits the face of the bat almost. Such intense concentration improves their chances of putting bat to ball, helps them time the ball better and gives them more time to play the ball. Good bowlers focus on the spot they want to pitch the ball to, as it improves accuracy and gives them time to make minor adjustments before they deliver the ball. Good fielders keep their eyes on the ball from the time it leaves the bat till it is safe in their hands; it improves their judgment, helps them complete the catch or make a proper stop. Whatever they do, cricketers learn to never take their eyes off the ball. The great ones concentrate that much more.

The highly talented Sanjay Manjrekar was coming off a wonderful season in university cricket with six back-to-back centuries and was already being hailed as the next big thing in Indian cricket; a worthy successor to Sunil Gavaskar. As a premier batsman in the country, one with impeccable technique and high degrees of concentration, he had the rare ability to leave balls that were even marginally outside the off stump. Very few batsmen I have bowled to have played the ball so late or left it so late. I remember feeling like a complete fool as he left ball after ball, aimed just a fraction outside the off stump.

Taking my eyes off the ball resulted in many painful consequences for me. While batting in the local league, I took my eyes off a short ball and paid with a broken nose on one occasion and a broken finger on another. Similarly, taking my eyes off the ball resulted in dropped catches, misfields, swollen fingers and other injuries, including a bruised ego. Much practice later, I learned to watch the ball all the way into my hands and hardly dropped any after. My newfound concentration helped me avoid much pain.

Coach's Corner

Concentrate fully on whatever you are doing. Hone your concentration to levels where nothing comes into your focus but the job at hand. The difference between ordinary work and excellence is the concentration you can bring to the job. Practice complete, undiluted focus.

No Ball

Hoping. Assuming. Cutting corners. Not seeing the details. Distractions. Taking things for granted.

The most famous stories about the virtue of concentration pertain to archery. In the *Mahabharata*, Dronacharya, the guru of the Pandava and Kaurava princes, invites all the princes for a test. They are asked to shoot the eye of a wooden bird hidden in a faraway tree with one single arrow. As they step up to take aim at the difficult target, he asks each one of them what they saw as their target. All princes reply that they could see various parts of the scenery, the tree, the branches and the bird. Drona tells them to step aside as they will not be able to hit the eye of the bird with such diffused concentration. In the end, Arjuna the great archer, says that he can see nothing else, but the eye of the bird and it is he who hits his target with one single arrow. Such is the concentration that is required of the masters.

I once asked one of the great Indian poets, a literary heavyweight, Padmashri awardee Shiv K Kumar, about the qualities a good writer needs to develop. Concentration, he said, is really the most important thing. I wondered then how concentration could be so important to writing. But as I wrote more, I realized how hard it is to keep a story or an article or a report hooked around the central theme without straying off track. I had to constantly guard against distracting ideas which led to many rewrites and trashed manuscripts. Keeping the eyes on the ball always helps to write clearly, precisely, confidently and convincingly.

Bonus Runs

When you bring concentration to work, the quality of your work deepens many times. It is the difference between greatness and mediocrity. It is also a great stress buster.

Exercise: Pick one small job for now – cleaning your keyboard or any such small thing you have been putting off. Work at it with complete concentration until you feel the perfection in your job. Be aware of the parts you felt like skipping, where you feel concentration flagging and refocus. Address that vague part with complete concentration and only then move on. Practice this level of concentration in all things.

---

15 | STABILITY

"If you accept your limitations you go beyond them."
– Brendan Francis

Taking guard. Knowing where your off stump is.

IT IS NOT ENOUGH TO KNOW where to focus your energies; it is equally important to know where you must not expend your energies. For batsmen, the area outside the off stump tests the best. It is the area of doubt, of temptation. Good batsmen do not flirt with stray deliveries that tempt them into poking at the ball from an unstable area. They leave alone those flirtatious deliveries that don't concern them and stay secure within their boundaries. Over time, they tire out bowlers and make them bowl in their area of control. They engage from a stable base and play within their limitations.

I remember watching a video of Rahul Dravid and Virender Sehwag bat against Jason Gillespie and Brett lee at the SCG during India's tour of Australia in 2004. There is one visual of Rahul Dravid as he leaves a ball from Jason Gillespie pitched outside the off stump in such a nonchalant manner that seemed to say – I don't need to engage with you at all. The next part of the innings shows Sehwag flirting with one delivery from Lee that is well outside the off stump. He edges it and is caught off a no ball. Soon after, another quick delivery outside the off stump and Sehwag flirts with it again, catch dropped by Ponting at slip. And again and again. At one end, we have Rahul Dravid all serene, secure and composed and wearing out the bowlers by wasting their effort, and at the other, there was Sehwag repeatedly going at balls that should have been left alone and getting Lee all fired up.

Coach's Corner

Be aware of your limits. Operate from within from a stable base – things that don't concern you, that are out of your area of control, draw energy and time away from what you need to concentrate on. Such distractions increase risk and lead to your downfall. If you wish to expand limits, do it bit by bit without compromising your stability. Playing within your limits improves control and consistency.

No ball

Greed. Haste. Overreaching. Injudiciousness. Imprudence.

Conflict between two countries (or even two people) is normally an outcome of one country reaching beyond the zone of its stability. If all countries stayed within their limits, there would be no war. But we have countries that poke at deliveries they have no business poking at. The USA was neutral to global conflict at the beginning of the World War II until Japan poked at the US base in Pearl Harbour without provocation. Enraged at the loss of life and property, USA entered the war. It was a move that changed the fortunes of the war as the Allies seized control. Japan paid a huge price for its unwarranted attack for years to come. It should not have played at harmless deliveries that did not concern it.

Similarly, in 1990, Iraq attacked and annexed its neighbouring country, Kuwait. This unprovoked move started a series of attacks on Iraq by USA led Allies and Kuwait was soon liberated from Iraq. It did not end there however. The seeds of war sown by Iraq led to further mayhem and destruction as USA attacked Iraq in 2003 and reduced the country into a further state of instability.

Iraq paid a high price for flirting with balls outside the off stump. Poor batting is all one can say.

I remember a senior colleague of mine, a highly qualified finance professional who worked in the bank. He worked harder than most and was considered one of those who would make it to the top. Imagine my surprise when he was fired from the job one day. It turned out he was passing on confidential information and making a fast buck. Another clerk lost his job for indulging in similar unscrupulous activities. In my days at the bank, I have seen many succumb to the lure of the temptation of loose deliveries outside the off stump.

My colleague and I chose two different paths while marketing our bank's products. He favoured an instable, high-risk approach of pulling strings and depending on favours or bribes to get some flashy big ticket clients. I believed I was better off doing what I know within my limitations. I called on prospects that had intrinsic strength, built my story and worked at it the hard way without falling for the lure of easy returns. My friend would laugh at me, because he'd get faster results. But after a year, my list of prospects converted into a solid client base that fetched good return, while his clients started defaulting and became problem cases.

Bonus Runs

Playing from a stable base reduces risk and improves consistency. It helps you achieve greater levels of success.

Exercise: Write down the major time-consuming activities you faced during the last three days along with the time spent on each activity. Tick the ones that concern your growth and cross out ones that do not. Calculate the time and energy you save for yourself by investing your energy for your own growth. The results will stagger you. Start investing those resources for your own growth. Leave those that don't help you grow.

---

16 | CONTROL

> "I cannot always control what goes on outside. But I can always control what goes on inside." – Wayne Dyer

Focus on what you can control.

EVER WONDER WHY SOME CRICKETERS deliver when the going gets tough and why some wither away when challenged? True champions deliver in all conditions. They do so because they focus on what they can control , such as their thoughts and their actions. They don't lose sleep and energy over the weather, opposition, umpires, media and such other things beyond their control. Sunil Gavaskar was called 'The Little Master', because he could bat on all sorts of wickets equally well. Glen McGrath was a handful to the best batsmen in the world on all surfaces. They focused on their game, their approach and their preparation.

Sunil Gavaskar's master class knock of 96 against Pakistan in Bangalore in 1987 on a minefield of a pitch comes to mind when you think of how he countered the uncontrollables by focusing on the controllables. It was a contest between the uncontrollable pitch and his technique and preparation. Most players mentally give up when they find a tough pitch to bat on, because they are already focusing on the uncontrollable factors. But champion players look at what's within their control, such as their game, their mind and their reactions, which is why they rise to the big occasion. That's how they back themselves to handle any condition.

The match was in the bag. We had scored 260. Our spinners got Hyderabad Allwyn down to 100 for 6. As their number eight walked in, we spotted dark clouds looming. We summoned the new ball, worried that rain would spoil our chances of a win, hoping to finish their tail off before it started raining. The spinners who were bowling well were taken off and fast bowlers were brought in. As our fast bowlers tried to bowl their overs quickly, the number eight batsman Maroof, got stuck into the shiny new ball and in a short while raced to his 50. The rain clouds disappeared and the rain never came. When Maroof hit the winning runs, the sun was shining gloriously and applauding. Big lesson! Don't bowl against the rain which is not in your control, bowl against the batsmen.

Coach's Corner

Act on what you can control. If nothing else, your thoughts and your actions are in your control. Uncontrollables drain energy and time. Controllables are work related. Action is in your control, but the result is not.

No Ball

Not doing the work. Worrying. Wasting time and energy over things you cannot control.

A Chinese saying: "When the archer shoots for no particular prize, he has all the skills; when he shoots to win a brass buckle, he is already nervous; when he shoots for a gold prize, he can't focus, sees two targets, and is out of his mind." Nothing is changing inside of you, only the stakes are getting bigger. Stop thinking of the what-ifs. Focus on your actions.

In Stephen R Covey's bestseller *The 7 Habits of Highly Effective People* comes the first habit – be proactive. Being proactive is about taking responsibility and focusing time and energy on things one can control. Dr Covey talks of the Circle of Influence and Circle of Concern. Proactive people focus efforts on the Circle of Influence and work on things they can do something about. Reactive people focus effort on the Circle of Concern, which is actually about things they have no control over. Dr Covey sure thought like a cricketer.

There were far too many factors to deal with in the tricky assignment. Watching our perplexed faces, our boss simplified things – "Let's do everything in our control first," he said, "Leave the rest to God". That made things simpler for us. We listed things in our control and got down to work – contacting agents, distributing marketing material, sending newsletters, filtering and meeting prospects. We left the major part of our job – worrying – to God. Since we had done all that we could do, and did it well (instead of trying to do everything), we ended up with brilliant results. Can't do more, can you? We did our part, God did his part.

Bonus Runs

When you focus on things you can control, there is less confusion and more control. There is better and measured response through deliberate action and non-action.

Exercise: Write down a situation that you worry about the most. Strike out the factors that are not in your control. Start working on the ones in control. Check the results. Life is easier and results get better.

---

17 | EQUANIMITY

"There is a huge amount of freedom that comes to you when you take nothing personally." — Miguel Ruiz

You win some, you lose some.

IT IS NOT EASY to take things in your stride when you are losing. Nor is it easy to be magnanimous when you are winning easily and think nothing can go wrong. But sooner or later cricketers learn to deal with ups and downs alike. They know that despite their best efforts, they cannot win all the time. The effort must go on despite failures, setbacks, rejections and criticism. It is this acceptance, that one must accept all hues of life in one's stride, that grows cricketers as people. One loss or even a series of losses will not break them.

One day you are champions and the next day you lose the first game; one innings you get a 100 and the next you are out first ball; one moment you are the hero and the next you are the villain, but you roll with the punches, smile, cry, and get along. You are toughened, hardened and wiser.

One of the most intriguing twists in the history of cricket comes from the life of Sir Donald Bradman. At the very end of a career that spanned 52 tests, 80 innings and 29 centuries, all he needed was a mere four runs to get that perfect batting average of 100 runs per inning in his illustrious Test career. The man who was said to have failed when he made a 50, walked in to bat against England at the Oval on August 14, 1948 to a standing ovation from a crowd of 30,000 and the sporting English team that surrounded him to say the three cheers. But on, the second ball , the Don was bowled by a googly from Eric Hollies. The shocking duck that silenced the entire stadium brought his average down to an agonizing 99.94. The Don never got a chance to play in the second innings, England being bowled out twice in that game. The Don's reaction – 'one of those things that happens in the game of cricket.' No one would have known better than the Don that cricket is about equanimity, taking the rough with the smooth. You win some, you lose some.

When I was dropped from the senior state side, I decided to quit the game and go back to my engineering. I was in my third year then, and decided not put any more energies into making a comeback. A few weeks later, I met someone who had seen much more of life than most and understood it well, ML Jaisimha. He told me, – "Life's not all about yesterday and today, Harry. There's always tomorrow." I never grasped what he meant then, wallowing in self pity as I was, but now I understand that he was urging me to practice what the game taught me. I did not in the past, but I do now.

Coach's Corner

Life has its ups and downs. Accept both and don't get attached only to the ups. If you have to get attached to something, get attached to effort. Purposeful effort will see you on the winning side more often. Go with the flow. Move on with the same disposition in all circumstances.

No Ball

Excessive attachment to results. Falling to pieces in adversity. Losing perspective in prosperity.

A zen story. A zen master was accused of impregnating a young girl from the village. When questioned by the irate villagers, the master merely said, "Is that so?" When the child was born, the outraged villagers left the child with him. They boycotted him. The Zen Master clothed, fed, sheltered and cared for the child. As the weeks went by, his reputation was destroyed in the village and beyond. The girl could take the guilt no longer and confessed that she was impregnated by someone else; she had lied about the monk. The villagers, filled with shame and regret, went to seek forgiveness. They also took the child away. Once again, the monk's only response was, "Is that so?"

While doing a course in vipassana, a Buddhist meditation technique, I understood what equanimity meant the hard way. Long hours of meditation got to me physically and mentally. My back and knees hurt, unaccustomed to the effort. But the technique teaches you not to twitch or move and instead, go deeper to focus your attention and awareness on the pain. It appeared highly unlikely that such a method would work. Imagine my surprise when the pain vanished as I focused my awareness on it. One moment it was there, and the other it was gone. The practice demonstrated that both pain and pleasure are transient. And when I saw the Buddhist monks deep in their meditation, their bodies radiating peace, awareness and acceptance, I knew that this too shall pass.

Bonus runs

Keep your perspective. Think long term. It helps you bounce back quickly.

Exercise: Look at the high points and the low points in your life where you are strongly attached to the outcome. Relive those moments. Is it possible to accept the result and move on? To look at the longer term? To let go? Apply them to a current situation. Practice non-attachment to the result. You will find that your life just got a lot easier.

18 | TACTICS

"All warfare is based on deception."
– Sun Tzu, The Art of Warfare

Do not show your emotions outwardly.

HOWEVER MUCH THEY MAY APPEAR like supermen, cricket captains are human too. Captains come in different packages: Some are highly passionate; they get too involved and curb the freedom and creativity of players with their intense and stifling micromanagement. Some are indifferent; no one in the team finds it inspiring to play under them as they do not appear concerned with the result anyway. Some are perfectionists; they put everyone on tenterhooks, because everyone is looking not to make mistakes.

When captains and players give themselves away to the opponents and their teammates through their emotions, pressure builds on the team. Has he given up?

Does he blame us? Is he angry? The best kinds of leaders are arguably, the ones who are cool and composed and make their team members feel that all is under control, even when everything on the ship is burning. The team somehow finds strength to focus on their job in such times. Such leaders keep calm and hold their cards close.

One of the greatest strengths of MS Dhoni is the air of complete control that he exhibits. It unnerves the opposition, because he seems to have a plan, some secret, even when there appears to be no way out for his team. His calm confidence seeps into his teammates, who find in themselves some inspiring spot and bowl a wicket-taking ball or hit a match-winning shot. They know their skipper has something up his sleeve and that they are a key part of the grand plan he has. As opponents guess, Dhoni's team gets the most unlikely players to come up with match-winning performances when least expected. What is it that Dhoni does? Nothing. He just keeps his emotions and thoughts to himself and looks like he has everything under control.

Sixty for eight chasing 180. We were done for. But our opponents, a young side, started panicking when our tenth wicket pair batted out five overs. Our two experienced players, opening batsmen Shameem and Ganesh, sensed the rising doubt, frustration and diminishing belief in the youngsters' minds and continued to play unhurriedly with no show of outward worry – calling for gloves, water, changing bats, etc. Perplexed at their behaviour, the opposition lost their cool, fought among themselves and eventually gave up, beaten in their own heads. Shameem got us a most unlikely win by scoring a 100. It was that uncertainty in the opponent's eyes that gave the game away for him, he confessed.

Coach's Corner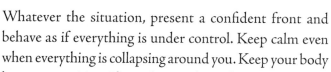

Whatever the situation, present a confident front and behave as if everything is under control. Keep calm even when everything is collapsing around you. Keep your body language positive. If you do not show that your pockets are empty, something gives.

No Ball

Extreme reactions. Tactical immaturity. Showing your cards prematurely.

In the Hindi film *Don* (1978), Amitabh Bachchan, the mafia boss, is trapped comprehensively by an avenging moll, Helen. She has emptied his revolver and the police have surrounded the hotel they are in, but Amitabh is cool as a cucumber as he examines his empty revolver carefully. Then he tells her impassively that only she and he know that the revolver is empty, but as far as the police are concerned, the revolver is loaded. He gags her, holds the empty gun to her head and walks off coolly under the noses of the police with his hostage. As long as you don't reveal that your gun is empty, people will believe that it is loaded.

My friend Suresh, who owns a global digital solutions company, recalls meeting a key prospect in California during his early days. Suresh badly needed that business and pitched his existing products and services hoping for a breakthrough. The prospect said that he did not need the products that Suresh offered. Instead, he had a requirement for another solution, one that Suresh and his team were still working on. Suresh did not miss a beat. He told the prospect that he would get the solution going in ten days. The deal was sealed. For the next ten days, Suresh worked three shifts a day with his team, and delivered a brand new solution. That one move opened up a new market and changed the course of the company as the delighted prospect referred the company's products to several new clients. Today, his company is a listed company that operates across the globe and employs over 500 employees. It's a story that hinged on that one moment when he chose not to show disappointment and instead, looked at the opportunity hidden behind it. It is not the empty gun, it is the possibility it offers and the conviction to carry it off and deliver. Most success stories are built on such hope and optimism; of empty guns that are fully loaded with a burning desire to make it work. What are you doing with yours?

My boss and I walked into a meeting with a tough customer with no sanction from our authorities in our pockets. I was nervous, but my boss looked as if he had everything under control. With little talk that gave nothing away, he conveyed to the customer that we had the best deal for him. So convincing was he that I wondered if he had already got the sanction to negotiate. The customer took the deal at a higher price than we were willing to settle for. "There is no need to tell them what they do not need to know. They only need to know what they think we can do," he told me later. Yes boss!

Bonus Runs

When you don't reveal your emotions, you put doubt in the opponent's mind and gain a psychological advantage. You win from no-win situations.

Exercise: List three situations you got upset in recently. Think of what would have happened in that situation if you had not got upset and kept your cool. The next time you catch yourself getting emotional, hold yourself. Go through it impassively. Say nothing, convey nothing. See how things change for the better. You will find that you're better off containing your emotions, especially if you are a leader.

---

19 | MASTERY

"Don't aim for success if you want it; just do what you love and believe in, and it will come naturally." – David Frost

Enjoy the process and success will follow.

CRICKETERS KNOW THAT THE ROUTE to sustained results is by enjoying the process. They train hard and let the process take over. "My subconscious mind knows exactly what to do. It is trained to react," says Sachin Tendulkar repeatedly.

All processes are laid out. A batsman knows that a big innings is built on a well-laid out process of settling in, minimizing risk, taking it ball by ball and session by session. A bowler follows the process of running in rhythmically, getting his action and follow through right, getting line and length, swing and seam right. Fielders follow the process of taking a start, keeping their eyes on the ball and are thus, able to deliver. The team follows a process of playing together, supporting one another, enjoying the pressure and giving their best effort to achieve a positive result. If one follows, trains and enjoys the process, one will relax, loosen up, enjoy the game and the pressure, gain mastery and most certainly, reap results.

During the T20 World Championships in 2012 in Sri Lanka, the world witnessed the spirit in which the West Indies played their cricket – dancing, celebrating, laughing and supporting one another. Clearly, the ones who enjoyed the process won. Such enjoyment is not mindless fun. When cricketers say they 'enjoy the process', they are enjoying the process of delving deeper into their craft and going into a meditative state – a space where they deliver high quality performances consistently.

We were playing against a strong East Zone varsities side at Varanasi in a Vizzy Trophy game in 1991. Encouraged by a green wicket, I got carried away and tried too much on the first day. Chasing our 220, the opponents were 60 for no loss. Next day, I told myself to focus on the process instead of trying to bowl fast. I relaxed, ran in at a balanced pace, held the seam upright and pitched the ball in the right areas – all the stuff involved in the process of good seam bowling. The more I focused on the process, the more I enjoyed it and the more the ball seamed. I got four early wickets in that morning spell

and we knocked the opponents over for a place in the final. We
won the Vizzy that year. Ah, the joys of enjoying the process.

Coach's Corner

True and lasting enjoyment comes from going deep into the
process and seeking mastery over it. If you are not enjoying
work, ask yourself this question – are you fully immersed in
it? Challenge your mastery over the process. Ask questions,
learn and clarify. Challenge kindles interest. Somewhere
along the journey, mastery becomes the goal. Results become
happy side effects. Immerse every cell 100 percent.

No Ball

Not knowing the process. Constant fear of failure.
Resentment. Superficial, half-hearted effort.

Musicians, dancers, actors and professionals show us
a glimpse of the divine when they immerse themselves
fully into the process. When we watch the maestros at
work, we know that true enjoyment of the process means
there is no labour as they deliver their performance. From
Bhimsen Joshi to MS Subbulakshmi, Michael Jackson to
U2, Placido Domingo to Luciano Pavarotti, the masters
transport audiences to a magical world. Do they appear

bored? No way. They appear to be lost in a love affair with their art, brimming with child-like anticipation at the enjoyment of performing.

Writing is hard work. Writing, typing, editing, sending proposals, facing rejection are all part of the process. In the end, much of what I write may never even get as much as a rejection slip. But there are times when I get so involved with the process that the mere thought of putting pen to paper, exploring an idea, developing it, refining it and sharing it becomes so interesting that I do it irrespective of the outcome. I lose all sense of time and effort. I seek to improve and to find that one idea that elevates the work. When we enjoy the process, we are giving our best, deliberately and lovingly. It is then not an effort, but a labour of love.

Bonus Runs

When you immerse yourself in the process, you enjoy it immensely. When you enjoy yourself, you are successful.

Exercise: List the things you work hard at but do not enjoy doing. What about it is not enjoyable to you? How much are you involved in it? Fifty percent? Seventy percent? Give in 100 percent to the process without worrying about the results or about others. You will start enjoying the process of learning.

---

20 | CREATIVITY

"Opportunities multiply as they are seized." – Sun Tzu

Catches win matches.

IT MAY APPEAR TO AN AMATEUR EYE that some of the greatest catches are more about luck than anything else; however, great catches are all about anticipation, optimism and technique. The best fielders create catches where none exist by being fully prepared, studying the batsman's strengths and weaknesses and anticipating the half chance that the batsman offers. It is a creative state of mind, where the individual is keen to take the attack to the opposition, conjure chances and make every mistake pay. Such players have the power to change the game. They create opportunities with their mindset.

From Eknath Solkar's full-length dive to grab a half chance by his finger tips to get rid of a stubborn Alan

Knott off Venkatraghavan at the Oval in 1971, a catch which they say changed the destiny of Indian cricket, to Jonty Rhodes flying sideways like a soccer goalie to get rid of Sachin Tendulkar in the final of the Tri-nation series in South Africa in 1997 – cricket's most interesting twists have always been orchestrated by opportunistic catches.

The best example in the context of the impact of a catch on a match is the one that Kapil Dev caught off Vivian Richards in the final of the 1983 World Cup. Richards, batting imperiously as only he can, crushed all hope of an Indian win until one mishit from his bat off Madan Lal rose into the air. It swirled high behind Kapil Dev and offered a glimmer of a chance. The Indian captain sensed opportunity, anticipated it, chased it and caught it, and turned the match decisively in that instant. India won the final and the World Cup in 1983. Kapil Dev's effort was the difference between hoping and actually making things happen.

Coach's Corner

You can make the most of every opportunity that comes your way if you are prepared for it. Anticipate opportunity, prepare yourself, expect the unexpected and convert half chances. Be aware. Take opportunities as they arise. The winning edge is about thinking ahead, creating chances and accepting opportunities as they come.

No ball

Dropping opportunities when they present themselves. Waiting for things to fall into your lap. Not acting on the moment. Postponing action.

Alexander the Great said that he did not wait for opportunities to come by, he created them. Young Alexander's armies were among the best prepared. From modified arms to sharp tactics, expert horsemanship to weapon training, his men were among the toughest and ablest. Alexander, who studied under the great philosopher Aristotle, was strategically superior and controlled the outcomes of war with far less damage to his armies and resources. As he surged across the continents conquering the world, Alexander followed the instincts of a master fieldsman and created opportunities that brought him many of his famous victories. These are exactly the sentiments that Jonty Rhodes would have echoed a few centuries later.

Closer home, Dhirubhai Ambani, who built the amazing story of the Reliance group, worked on one principle – anticipate and be prepared for opportunity. Starting out with almost nothing in his pocket, Dhirubhai went to Aden, Yemen, to work as a gas station attendant for A. Besse & Co, a distributor of Shell products. While working there, he picked up a sense of trade and returned to India to trade in spices. He sensed opportunity in manufacturing and set up a textile unit in Ahmedabad. In 1966, he founded Reliance Industries, a company that shaped the fortunes of India's equity markets, investors and many industrial sectors and is listed among the Fortune 500 companies of the world. To achieve so much in one lifetime is not possible without creating opportunity and making the most out of it when it presents itself. From envisioning demand, creating ways to open locked up capital and accessing it and finding efficiencies to satisfy shareholders year after year, Dhirubhai scripted a superstar journey in Indian corporate markets.

We negotiated a big deal with a giant pharmaceutical company. However, the company backed off at the last minute and cancelled the deal. Our team was completely devastated, but my boss saw an opportunity in that situation. He got an approval from our authorities for the deal, just in case the company changed its mind and agreed to our terms. Despite no real chance of getting that deal, we prepared from our side as if we were going to get it. Miraculously, the company called up after three months and asked us if our offer was open. They needed funds desperately and were agreeable to our terms. We were ready and grabbed the opportunity with both hands.

That one deal catapulted us into the top performers of the year. My boss, though a non-cricketer, showed all the signs of an expert short leg fielder, as he anticipated the opportunity and grabbed it when it came.

Bonus Runs

Being creative opens up opportunities that do not exist otherwise. It helps you prepare, anticipate and think ahead. It opens up a new world of possibilities.

Exercise: List out all the opportunities you missed or did not accept when they came your way. Then, list all those opportunities that you anticipated and created. Are you dropping more or catching more? Start preparing for opportunities as if they are coming your way. Create opportunities instead of waiting for them. Accept them when they come your way. You'll see a marked progress in your life.

---

21 | WILLINGNESS

"The amount of good luck coming your way depends on
your willingness to act." – Barbara Sher

Take the first run fast. Every run counts.

TO PLAY WITH THE SLIGHTEST reluctance or distraction
is to surrender a big advantage. To the batsman who
is willing, a world of opportunities opens up. Batsmen
run the first run fast to push for extra runs should the
possibility arise. Every run adds a crucial advantage. Top
teams convert singles into twos and twos into threes,
making the most of every opportunity.

The key to these precious extra runs is the willing
mindset of batsmen to run the first run fast, whatever the
outcome of the shot may appear to be. The ball may be up
in the air for an easy catch, it may look like it is heading
for a certain boundary or a seemingly non-existent second

run, but batsmen have to do their job and run like hell. In the event the catch gets dropped, the ball is stopped or the fielder fumbles, an extra run is possible.

It was a close Australia versus India match in the 1992 World Cup game at Brisbane. India needed four runs to win off the last ball with the last wicket pair at the crease. Javagal Srinath, on strike against Tom Moody, swung hard and connected. The ball sailed high towards the mid-wicket boundary. Non-striker, number 11 batsman, Venkatapathi Raju ran towards Srinath congratulating him. "I thought he had hit a six. I did not realize that the wind was so stiff that the ball dropped into Steve Waugh's hands," said Raju in retrospect. Srinath, who saw the ball ballooning in the stiff wind, urged Raju to keep running. Steve Waugh dropped the catch, recovered and threw the ball in. But Raju's first run was not the fastest owing to his slowing down to congratulate Srinath and it compromised the second run. He was run out attempting the third, which could have tied the game. Australia won by one run. If only Raju had run the first run fast!

In an ODI against England, MS Dhoni and Suresh Raina ran two runs where none existed. The ball deflected off Dhoni's pads and went down the leg side to the wicketkeeper who threw at the stumps, creating one extra run. Dhoni ran the first run like lightning and turned to see the wicketkeeper still lying on the ground some ten feet away and the ball near the stumps. He assessed the risk, turned and ran the second run even as a hapless wicketkeeper desperately tried to make amends. Two precious extra runs were added where none existed. You cannot keep such a sense of optimism and opportunism down.

Coach's Corner

Show your willingness in every act and thought. Grab every chance. Accumulate the small change. It indicates that you want to make the most of every opportunity. Say yes to life. Nothing is too small to matter.

No Ball

Being complacent. Saying no to life. Being casual about small things. Unwilling to work hard when no guaranteed result is seen.

It is said that every self-made millionaire first learns the art of being thrifty. Thomas J Stanley is someone who has studied the habits of self-made millionaires closely and has authored the popular books *The Millionaire Next Door*, *The Millionaire Mind* and *Millionaire Women Next Door*.

His books give out some interesting facts about self-made millionaires who are early risers, often drive used cars, clip grocery coupons, live in middle-class homes, mend their own clothing, re-upholster furniture and search for foreclosed homes. He says in *The Millionaire Next Door,* "What are the three words that profile the affluent? Frugal, frugal and frugal." Famous cases include Warren Buffet, the most successful investor of the 20th century and one of the world's wealthiest men, who still lives in his old 1958 USD 31,500 home in Omaha; Michael Bloomberg of Bloomberg LP valued at USD 22.5 billion, who owns two well-worn loafers; and David Cheriton, one of the founder-investors in Google with a net worth of USD 1.3 billion, who reportedly saved half his meals from expensive restaurants to eat at home the next day and has been his own barber for the past 15 years. There is much evidence that every run counts.

At my favourite music store in Hyderabad as a 15-year-old, I remember one particular salesman who treated every single customer with care and respect. As I stood at the back, gazing longingly at the album covers, he made the extra effort to show me new music, play it and suggest alternatives. Over time, he sold many new albums to me and converted me into a happy and loyal customer. I go to that store even now, 25 years later, and he is still his old enthusiastic self. He taught me how to do the small things well, because every extra bit counts in the long run. Every single customer counts.

Bonus Runs

Your work gets recognized when you show willingness to do the small things well. Your willing approach opens the way to new responsibilities. By being willing, you constantly add value to yourself and grow.

Exercise: List out the small units or processes in your job. Accumulate expertise in these basic units. Notice how your work gets recognized when you show willingness to do the small things well. Be willing to accept any responsibility. Say yes to jobs that need you to go out of your way and add value even through seemingly small jobs.

As a habit, start using 'yes' more often than 'no' when you speak. See if the outcomes change.

---

22 | RESPONSIBILITY

"The price of greatness is responsibility." – Winston Churchill

Take 100 percent responsibility. Finish what you began.

PLAYING WINNING CRICKET IS ALL about responsibility. Though every member in the team has a clear responsibility spelt out for him, it is understood that the person who has got a start must carry on and finish the job. They walk that extra mile to finish the game even if they are tired or in discomfort. They do not leave things to the next person however small the job left. When you are in, it's your responsibility to complete the job. That's the reason you're there. An irresponsible shot even at the end of a big 100 is not appreciated in the dressing room.

Needing a mere 17 runs to win with three wickets in hand in the Chennai Test against Pakistan in 1999, India was almost home. Sachin Tendulkar was batting on 136, a masterful innings. However, a persistent back pain got the better of his concentration and Sachin holed out, trying to loft Saqlain Mushtaq after restraining himself for long. Inexplicably, the rest of the batting caved in and India lost a match it could have won. Despite having done 90 percent of the job, Sachin's glorious knock went in vain. It is the kind of match that stays in your mind all your life – why did I not finish the job, you think. Coaches tell their wards the very same thing – if you have got a start, complete the job.

On a happier note, in 1998, in two innings of exemplary responsibility, Sachin Tendulkar scored back-to-back centuries, 143 and 134, against a tough Aussie attack and almost single-handedly ensured an Indian title win over Waugh's Australians.

Kapil Dev was dropped for one Test match against England in Delhi in 1984, the only time in his illustrious career that he was dropped, for playing what was considered an irresponsible shot. The same Kapil Dev, however, displayed all the responsibility in the world when he scored an unbeaten 175 against Zimbabwe to lift a struggling India from 17 for 5 to an improbable win in the 1983 World Cup. On another occasion, he smote Eddie Hemmings for four consecutive sixes to avoid the ignominy of a highly probable follow on with only one wicket in hand. Responsibility and desire to win go hand in hand.

It was a league match at the Khursheed Jah grounds in the Old City of Hyderabad in 1995. We bowled the opposition out for 123 and were cruising at a healthy 107 for 4. The stylish Chandrasekharan and I were batting with 34 and 30 apiece and were heading for a comfortable win. With 17 runs to get, I decided that I had done enough, heaved wildly, and got out, caught at mid-wicket. Satisfied with my cameo, I watched the match from the sidelines, hoping to celebrate a win soon. But in an astonishing collapse, the next five batsmen got out for a mere ten runs and returned to join me. We lost. If the Indian selectors who had dropped Kapil Dev were watching that shot, I'd have surely been dropped for the next game. I kick myself even today for not finishing the match myself.

Years later, when we were 20 for 6 chasing 125 in another game, I scored an unbeaten 54, and helped our side win. Taking on that responsibility felt really good. I felt that I could handle anything after that.

Coach's Corner

Take 100 percent responsibility and finish what you begin. See your vision through. Once you learn how to finish a job, you become a valuable asset to any team. Take up greater responsibility at every opportunity and deliver to satisfaction. This is the path to growth.

No Ball

Being easily satisfied. Taking partial responsibility. Ninety-nine percent responsibility is not good enough, 100 percent is required. Being lazy. Not pushing limits. Not finishing what you began. Blaming others for not finishing your job.

Remember the popular children's story of 'The Little Dutch Boy'? It is a story of a school boy who spots a leak in a dike in Holland. Seawater was trickling in and there was no one around to help. So, the boy puts his finger in the leak to avoid the impending disaster of seawater flooding the city. He stayed up in the cold all night until help arrived the next morning. That is what 100 percent responsibility is about. The boy did not leave the leak and run away. He took the responsibility of preventing a flood upon his own shoulders.

Selling nailing machines to defence organizations around Pune, I had lined up an important demo. I asked our technical team to help with the demo, while I focused on my sales pitch. On the big day, the main technical guy did not show up and sent his new assistant instead. When the top brass of the client came to see the demo, the rookie fumbled and could not get the machine working in time. The exercise was a colossal flop. I lost a golden opportunity to sell a few hundred machines, just because I had left the most important part to the technical team. If I wanted to finish the job, I could have learned how to use the machine and conduct the demo myself.

Bonus Runs

Your growth is related to the responsibilities you are willing to take. When you accept more responsibilities, you grow faster.

Exercise: Make a list of all the things you are leaving for other people to finish for you (and the things happening in your life that you are blaming them for). Make two columns. In the first, write all that you are doing to handle your current level of responsibility. In the second, write what else you need to do if you were to take 100 percent responsibility and finish those jobs (this is the stuff you are leaving for others to do). Take charge of the second column and see how jobs get done.

---

23 | RESILIENCE

"Greatest glory in living
lies not in never falling,
but in rising every time we fall." – Nelson Mandela

Fall, but rise.

ALL OF US FACE TWO CHOICES all our life – to hang on and face adversity or give up. The ones who hang on without running away become the heroes. Hit by a Merv Dillion delivery in the Antigua Test in 2002, Anil Kumble fractured his jaw and was scheduled to fly back to Bangalore for surgery. But the combative spinner returned to the field with his broken jaw wired up, bandaged and snared the vital wicket of Brian Lara. Dean Jones in a marathon double hundred made at Chennai in 1986 was down, as he sweated, vomited and cramped, but he kept on going in the 42 degree celsius Chennai heat. Malcolm

Marshall, the great West Indian fast bowler, batted one-handed with a broken thumb and helped Larry Gomes complete his century. He then returned in a Test match at Headingley against England in 1984 to bowl with his hand in a cast, and claimed 7 for 53 with one good hand. West Indies won.

In the 1976 series between England and West Indies, Brian Close took the frightening pace of the West Indian bowlers to his body and continued to doggedly stand up, resulting in an iconic picture of the bruises on his battered body taken later in the dressing room. Teams like India have risen from being dead and buried to winning, as in the 2001 Calcutta Test when India came back from a follow on and won. Resilient players made many comebacks after being dropped – Mohinder Amarnath comes instantly to mind. You can knock them down, but you cannot keep them out. Resilience is mental.

It would be foolish to think that cricket is always the gentleman's game. As in every other place, there are enough rogue elements here. All attacks are not straight. From slurs to abuse, Machiavellian conspiracies to assault, all kinds of crimes have been perpetrated on and off the field. No cricketer is blind to all the unfairness that goes on behind the scenes, but they let their game do the talking for them. They do not let these underhand tactics bother or break them, knowing that the last man standing has the last laugh. They find ways to deal with the dirt, come through and do not succumb.

I have seen some stirring displays of resilience and character, but none as vivid as my friend D Suresh's innings against TNCA in a Buchi Babu match at Chepauk. His nose was broken early in his innings by a well-directed bouncer and he was sent off for repairs. Suresh came back with his nose bandaged, eyes as narrow slits, his handsome face swollen and bruised. We thought he was out of the game, but he padded up and went in to bat with our side in a bit of a bother, only to be hit in the exact spot again with the first ball – same bowler, same bouncer. Luckily, he was wearing a helmet this time around and it dented the grill. If the opponents thought he would back off, they had another thing coming – the next ball went sailing over point for a flat six. In a stirring counter attack, Suresh got 97 of the best that I have seen under pressure, and blitzed the strong TNCA side out of the game.

Coach's Corner

Get up, even if you fall. Quitting is the easiest thing. There will be tough times and unfair times, but if you get back on your feet, you will overcome them in the end. Keep coming back until you get it.

No Ball

Low commitment. Quitting. Giving up early. Showing no fight. Falling apart at the first hit.

Viktor E Frankl, most famous for his book *Man's Search for Meaning*, survived three years at concentration camps during the Second World War. The war claimed his pregnant wife, his parents and a brother, but Frankl bounced back from those horrific memories, married again, worked as a professor of neurology and psychiatry at the University of Vienna Medical School, wrote 32 books that have been translated into 26 different languages. Viktor E Frankl's life symbolizes resilience at its best.

Running after all the publishers of the world with my first manuscript (still unpublished by the way) and coping with their rejections did not put me off writing. I must mention here that each rejection does feel a bit like a boxer's upper cut that knocks you off your feet – a bit like being rejected in love. I brushed it off, tried more publishers and received more rejections. Okay, I told myself, I get the message. I wrote another book. I got a publisher this time, but he had no money and no plan. After two years, we parted ways. Okay, write another. Finally, one publisher bought it. Eight years since the first rejection, I got the first book published. If you keep coming back, they cannot keep you out forever. It's only a question of when.

Bonus Runs

You will get what you want in the end or even something better, if you don't give up.

Exercise: What is the one job that makes you feel like giving up now? Write down the difficulties you may encounter on the path. At each difficulty decide that you will keep coming back and develop a game plan. You will prevail finally.

---

24 | GRACE

"Grace is the absence of everything that indicates pain or difficulty, hesitation or incongruity." – William Hazlitt

Follow through.

IT'S IN THE PROPER CLOSURE of any act that one experiences grace. In cricket, a good bowling action is one that finishes strongly with a robust follow through. To the uninitiated, a follow through is the completion of any action fully and the graceful slowing down of momentum of the body. Watch fast bowling legends and their bowling actions in their most destructive spells. Michael Holding follows through like the wind as he decimates England in a superb display of fast bowling at the Oval in 1976. Dennis Lillee rips the heart out of England in the 1977 Centenary Test at the same venue. Bob Willis runs through Australia at Headingley in 1981 for his 8 for 43 and Malcolm Marshall steams in against England at Old Trafford in 1988. In full flow, they do not stop abruptly after bowling. They finish powerfully, gracefully and end up within handshaking distance of the batsmen by the time they finish their follow through. Much of their pace, direction and control comes from their resolute follow through.

The follow through after the shot while batting or after the throw while fielding adds control, power, direction and beauty to the act. When cricketers pull up short without finishing the action, the result is abrupt, uncoordinated and imprecise. But when one envisions the entire act, including a smooth follow through, it becomes a graceful, powerful and form of art. It is what makes it all look so beautiful to watch.

My first coach, the best I ever had, was Mr Rehmat Baig, then a BCCI coach. It was my first year at school cricket and I was raw, to put it mildly. The first few balls that I bowled were enough for Mr Baig to pull me aside for special treatment. He asked me to bowl and follow through. I did, and promptly fell, thanks to an unhealthy habit of locking my follow through with one leg. It took many awkward falls to correct the mistake, but once it was rectified, I could see the difference it made to my bowling. I was an entirely different proposition.

Coach's Corner

Whatever you start, follow through resolutely. The follow through is an integral part of the action, not an add-on that you can skip. It adds sting to your entire act. Do not give up abruptly at the first sign of trouble at whatever you begin. A committed follow through maximizes the potential of your effort. When you are committed, your act will never be halfhearted, it will be graceful. Be it a business, a relationship, a job or a negotiation, follow through for best results.

No Ball

Abrupt, halfhearted efforts. Giving up too soon. No proper closure.

All successful stories are products of a good follow through. The fledgling company Infosys almost came to an abrupt stop in 1989, unwilling to follow through. It looked like it was going nowhere and the dejected team wanted to stop, because their efforts had not produced sufficient results. But Mr Narayana Murthy, like an expert cricketer, knew the importance of following through, and told the others categorically that the business would continue, even without the others. Except for one, the team stayed back. The amazing Infosys story benefited from the fine and resolute follow through of Mr Narayana Murthy, who did not wish to halt the momentum that Infosys had already built up. He was certainly thinking on the lines of Lillee, Holding and Steyn.

When a business prospect told me that he'd never do business with our bank because of some earlier unpleasantness, I suspended all further interaction with him abruptly. But my boss insisted that since I had initiated action, I better follow up and keep the momentum going. A day came, after two years of seemingly pointless meetings, when the client asked me if I could match an offer from a competing supplier. My boss and I followed it up, persisted through many glitches and brought that client into our fold. If I'd stopped abruptly after the first meeting without the necessary follow through, we'd have never got that important wicket.

Bonus Runs

Following through in every situation adds grace, gives direction, completes things and brings unexpected results. You make a lasting impression.

Exercise: List all your unfinished jobs. Would they have reached a logical conclusion if you had followed them up without making your own assumptions? Commit to following them up and completing them. Adopt that attitude of following through properly to the end. Observe the results. You will find unexpected avenues opening up. Following up closes the loop gracefully.

25 | SELF-ACCEPTANCE

"Because one believes in oneself, one doesn't try to convince others. Because one is content with oneself, one doesn't need others' approval. Because one accepts oneself, the whole world accepts him or her." – Lao Tzu

Know yourself and your game to achieve your potential.

WE BLOSSOM FULLY WHEN we recognize our unique nature and allow ourselves to be who we truly are. Saurav Ganguly's timing, Sehwag's aggression, Rahul Dravid's ability to play long innings – they knew their nature and their game well. If, instead, Sehwag tried to play defensively like Dravid or if Dravid tried to be aggressive like Sehwag, they might not have been as successful as they were. Sachin Tendulkar's bottom-handed grip was the subject of many a discussion by cricket pundits, but he knew his game and persevered. For that matter, players with unconventional actions like Mike Proctor, Phillip De Freitas, Lasith Malinga, Paul Adams and the like did not try to change to conventional styles. It's important to know your essence, accept it and remain true to it.

The day I accepted that winning was important to me and things changed. I found no need to be nice or politically correct. I stopped trying to hide my weaknesses. I accepted my strengths. I felt no shame in asking for help. I was not apologetic anymore. All I wanted to do was win. The moment I accepted it, the results showed. This self-acceptance worked wonders for me at the inter-university games, the Vizzy Trophy, the Sunday league Championships, table tennis matches, the Times Shield matches, in my academics and in my work in the corporate sector – the new attitude seeped into every aspect of my life and gave it a sharp edge.

Coach's Corner

Accept yourself as you are whole and complete with the good and the bad. It takes a lot of pressure off you. Stop being apologetic about yourself. When you have nothing to hide, you stop worrying about other people and their opinions. Your ease will reflect in your performance positively. When you accept your true nature, you will stop resisting. You move forward towards your potential.

No Ball

Being defensive about yourself. Imitating others. Being someone you are not. Not accepting certain parts of yourself. Saying you know when you don't and consequently, hindering your own growth.

In the movie *Cool Runnings* (1993), loosely based on a true story, Sanka Coffie, the hero and Derise's friend, puts his foot down in a defining moment. Noticing his friend besotted with the champion Swiss team and how he was trying to behave like them, Sanka tells him that since they are Jamaicans, they will be and play like Jamaicans – be it their clothes, their approach, their dance or their attitude to life. "We have our own style," he says. "The best I can be is Jamaican... we look Jamaican, walk Jamaican, talk Jamaican and is Jamaican. Then we sure as hell better bobsled Jamaican." Once the team accepts that they are best as they are, the smiles come on, the swagger comes on, the looseness and coolness comes on, and they put on a fine performance that brings them back into the reckoning as outside favourites.

When I first started writing, I remember imitating authors that I admired – Wodehouse for one – and whoever else I was reading at that time. I realized soon that I had to be myself if I wanted to get anywhere as a writer. Find my voice, as they say. Who was I? What was I? Was I stylish, funny or irreverent? As I wrote more, I discovered a voice in me that was simple and straight, direct and frank. I stuck to it. Writing is much simpler now. I do not feel the pressure to be someone else, to impress, to write flowery phrases, unusual metaphors, etc. I tell the story as it is, as honestly and as directly as I can. I think that's me and I am comfortable in my shoes. In any other voice, however impressive, I know I am playing a role.

Bonus Runs

Accepting yourself fully as you are is the best way forward. When there is nothing to hide, there is everything to gain.

Exercise: Write down all that you are proud of about yourself, your achievements, skills, etc. Then, write down all that you are ashamed of, things you feel you are not and things you do not want to accept about yourself. Accept both. If there is any resistance to accept any part, figure out why. Be willing to accept that part, too. Once you accept all parts, take the new unapologetic you to work and see the difference. You will move forward faster than most.

---

26 | SELF-BELIEF

"You have to believe in yourself before anybody else believes in you." – Ray LaMontagne

Back your ability fully.

THERE ARE TIMES WHEN WE FEEL we can do anything; it comes out of some crazy self-belief. If only we could back ourselves with that confidence more frequently, we might achieve so much more. Young Tendulkar stepped up confidently to take the ball from skipper Azharuddin's hands and bowl the last over against the Proteas in the Hero Cup semifinal in 1993-94. South Africa needed a mere six runs to win and Kapil Dev and Srinath still had two overs left with them. Sachin Tendulkar's first over of the match went for an incredible three runs and India won against all odds. This was self-belief of the highest order. MS Dhoni frequently backs himself to win duels off the last over against the best bowlers – his 16 in four balls against Sri Lanka in the Tri-series in the West Indies in 2013 against Eranga is one among many that he pulls off. Champion cricketers fare well in tight circumstances, because they believe in themselves.

Indian cricketer and now commentator, Ravi Shastri, is another fine example of how self-belief is more important to be successful than mere talent. Starting out as a young left arm spinner and a lower order batsman who batted at number nine, Ravi Shastri worked his way up by sheer application and self-belief and became one of India's leading all-rounders, performing above his weight at crucial times and scoring centuries as an opener against the toughest bowling attacks in the world. Self-belief is that feeling of I-can-handle this. It's not ability, it is about capability.

Bolstered by the presence of model, swimmer, all-round sportsman and now television commentator Charu Sharma, the VST team ran up a daunting total of 350 runs in 90 overs. Something clicked in my mind as we walked off the field. I requested my captain DTS Prasad to let me open the innings and promised him that I would score 128 runs, the number of runs I had given away in that innings in my bowling. For me, it was one of those I-can-do-it moments. He agreed. For someone who normally batted at number eight, I backed myself to get runs in that pressure game and scored

158. Our score was 266 for 4 when I got out. We won the match. One sharp chance was all I gave when I was on 28. My friend Charu dropped it at the gully, but otherwise, it was flawless. After that knock, I started to believe that I could do anything – even writing a novel.

Coach's Corner

Believe in what you have. Whatever you have right now is enough for you to handle anything that comes up. Back your ability with self-belief. Miracles will occur. Volunteer for big challenges. Tell yourself – I can handle this. You will find a way.

No Ball

Worrying about what you don't have. Looking for excuses. Looking outside for help. Not accepting challenges. Saying no to growth opportunities. Listening to those who diminish your self-belief.

In the story of David and Goliath, young David, a water carrier in the war, displayed immense self-belief in taking on the giant Goliath in a single combat to decide the outcome of the battle. This was a challenge thrown by Goliath that no soldier took up. Refusing armour, young David took his stick, a sling and five stones to battle, attacked a fully armed Goliath on his forehead and felled him. Young David won not because of a lucky shot, it was the self-belief that he could do it that sealed it.

In my first sales job, I felt like a complete misfit. My colleagues were a bunch of suave, smooth, slick talkers, wheeling-dealing their way through the sales process, by hook or by crook. I was awkward and unsure, and could do none of the things they could, so I asked myself what I could do. One thing I could do was turn in an honest, diligent performance (read as dumb in sales parlance). I decided to back what I had and forget about what I did not have. I scanned the client list and noticed that we had a mediocre list of clients – not a single A list client. I decided to go after the elusive top 20 companies. My colleagues and my boss laughed at my lofty ambitions, but after a year of dedicated and committed work, I managed to bring 18 of the top 20 clients into our fold and with them, rock solid, long-term business. I merely backed myself, my capability and my method, and did not pay heed to the negative talk. I was the star performer that year.

Bonus Runs

When you do it once, you know you can do it again. Your self-confidence goes up when you back yourself to do things and achieve them.

Exercise: Write down all the areas that you think you cannot handle with your current abilities, especially the areas where you doubt yourself for no apparent reason. Take the challenge. Tell yourself strongly that you can handle those areas successfully. Take full responsibility, leave no scope for escape and find a way to handle them – and you will. It's one decision away in the mind. You can handle it.

27 | COMMITMENT

"Live as if you were to die tomorrow. Learn as if you were to live forever." – Mahatma Gandhi

Think long term. Commit forever.

IN AN IDEAL WORLD, no batsman would ever want to get out. But in the real world, the thought of batting on and on forever can tire you, bore you and make you do silly things and get out. That is not what true commitment or true batsmanship is about. The best come to the crease with a commitment to bat till the end of the inning and remain unbeaten every time. This mindset commits them to the cause, and places responsibility on them. On the other hand, there are batsmen who do not show any commitment (the tail enders more so), live dangerously and perish easily. To commit mentally to the longest term requires batsmen to plan their innings, to survive, to adapt, to manage mental fatigue and sustain concentration. When time is taken out of the picture, clarity sets in.

In an epic innings played at Johannesburg against South Africa in 1995, Michael Atherton, batted over two days, 643 minutes, faced 492 balls for a fighting 185 not out and saved England from defeat. Atherton later said that it was an innings that defined him. Needing an improbable 479 to win in the final innings, England was 167 for 4 at the end of the fourth day. As he batted stubbornly on and on, Atherton, in what was described as an over-my-dead-body innings, said that at one point, he was in the zone. "I was in an almost trance-like state. It was a state of both inertia and intense concentration and I knew that I was in total control and they couldn't get me out." Commitment means forever. Commitment makes you transcend the ordinary.

The same thought resonated with our team, when we committed ourselves to winning the South Zone trophy for Osmania University in 1991. All else faded when we committed ourselves – effort, time, reputation and petty differences. All that mattered was to get it right. There was no scope for excuses, for not achieving what we committed ourselves to. When that thought drops in, there is no question of failing. We won.

Coach's Corner

Take time out of the equation. Commit for the longest term in all that you take up (even if it's a short-term job). When you work at something with the attitude of a lifetime commitment, it brings a whole new perspective to the quality of work. You utilize your resources optimally.

No Ball

Impatience. Boredom. Fatigue. Giving up. Shortcuts and escape routes.

That stubborn thought entered Dashrath Manjhi, now famously known as the 'Mountain Man', who single-handedly dug a 360 ft long and 30 ft wide road through Geholour hills in Bihar. Manjhi dug that road after his wife died due to lack of access to medical treatment. The nearest doctor was 70 km away, beyond the mountain. Manjhi did not want anyone else in his village to suffer the same fate as his wife and started digging a tunnel, one stone at a time. His individual commitment, working day and night for 22 years (from 1960 to 1982), reduced the distance between the Atri and Wazirganj blocks in Gaya district from 55 km to 15 km. Once Manjhi committed himself to the Herculean task, time and effort had no meaning; it was a matter of when, not if.

Following his example, Ramchandra Das dug a tunnel in a mountain for 14 years to complete a 10 m long and 4 m wide tunnel from his village to Kewati. He had asked the authorities to build a tunnel connecting his village to the road. When they refused, he decided to do it himself, using only a hammer and a chisel.

In Gabriel Garcia Marquez's *Love in the Time of Cholera*, Florentino Ariza waits 58 years for his loved one, Fermina Daza. Such commitment cannot be denied. Ariza keeps his long vigil alive by keeping track of his love and arranging accidental meetings. He finally convinces a 70-year-old Fermina on a romantic cruise, after she is widowed. Ariza's love would appear similar to the commitment of batsmen who score those big triple hundreds.

A student of mine once asked me how to sustain his effort at losing weight. Every once in a while he gets motivated to work out but after a few days, he loses steam and gives up. I did not know the answer when he asked me at first. On deeper thought, all I could think of was that one should commit to such things for a lifetime, not merely do them for a lark. Commit to exercising first thing in the morning for the rest of your life. Once time is out of the picture and there is no escape, you settle down to do the work.

In corporate meetings, I learned from true professionals how they take time out of the equation and commit to a resolution, however long the meetings may run. Some experienced foxes use that strategy to mentally wear out the younger ones by dragging meetings for long and ungodly hours. To beat them, you need to commit for the longest time, so the mind does not wander and lose concentration. When you are committed to your task, be prepared to outlast everyone.

Bonus Runs

When you commit to something, it is a matter of when, not if. You will get what you want, or even something better. You plan and execute better.

Exercise: The next time you are faced with a job that makes you uncomfortable and less confident, commit yourself to sit through it however long it may take. Use the switch on and switch off mode to keep your concentration high. To do a good job, keep time out of the equation. You may lose a few battles, but you will win the war.

---

28 | BELIEF

Belief creates the actual fact. – William James

What you believe, you experience.

TO HOLD ONTO YOUR BELIEF is to create the reality you want. When the stakes pile up, the champions hold onto their belief, while the losers simply give up. It seemed all over for Australia in the semifinal of the 1999 World Cup. Lance Klusener smashed eight of the nine runs required to win off Damien Fleming's first two balls in such emphatic fashion that the match was as good as over. But Aussie skipper Steve Waugh did not lose belief in himself or his team. He surrounded Klusener with all his fielders, saving the solitary run left to get. The Aussie belief that they could still pull it off affected Klusener's rhythm and instead of trusting his natural instinct and attacking, he decided to take a single. Allan Donald was run out. With the scores tied, Australia made it to the final based on its earlier win over South Africa in the league stage. Belief can be stronger than steel if you can hold onto it. Waugh held on, Klusener let go.

Defending a low total of 183 in the World Cup final in 1983, Kapil Dev did not lose his belief. He reminded his team that the West Indians had to get the runs on the board. It was a statement that exemplified his belief that they were still in the game. Perhaps, the team may have thought, we could win. The rest is history.

Playing our old rivals Sacred Heart CC at their home ground, we were skittled out for 110. Our first two overs cost 20 runs. Many of our own supporters wrote us off, but we believed that we could beat them somehow. Sreenu's second over got us two wickets. Two stunning catches at short leg by Pavan and the opponents were down to 21 for 4. A rare, intense energy spread throughout the team. We shot them out for 90. Sreenu got a well-deserved five-wicket haul and I got the other five. We celebrated big time that day with Chandra throwing a party none of us will ever forget. That day, only our collective belief pulled us through. We did not get in the way of that belief and that's all.

Coach's Corner

Belief is a thought. Pay attention to your belief and you can create the results you want. Your belief will always prove you right. Believe in people and they will deliver. Believe in yourself and you can move mountains. When you believe, miracles happen. Hold onto your belief even when the stakes rise against you. Miracles happen.

No Ball

Lack of belief in oneself and others. Excuses, blame and criticism. Poor results. Weak belief that collapses in adversity.

In the movie *Kung Fu Panda* (2008), Po's father, Mr Ping the goose, who owns a noodle restaurant, reveals the secret ingredient of his famous noodle soup to his son: "Nothing," he squawks. "There is no secret ingredient." Po is surprised. "Nothing?" he asks perplexed. Mr Ping replies that he does not add anything. "Don't have to," he says, "to make something special, you just have to believe it's special." Po remembers these words when he looks at his reflection in the dragon scroll – nothing, but himself. All he has to do is believe that he is the dragon warrior and he will be. That, is the power of belief.

I never had a job in my hand when I left the previous one. All I had was a belief that I could land the one I wanted. When I finally left my banking career to choose a writing career, I had little to support that decision as well, save sheer belief (and Shobha's unwavering support). This belief is not the self-belief in my capabilities, but a belief that the universe that created me will sustain me and my choice to express myself in the best manner possible. Not having a job with the perks and the comforts jobs bring, not being a sought-after writer where publishers chase you with large advances does not matter. It is only the belief in what made me that sustains this enterprise. That something, somehow, will sustain the magic.

Bonus Runs

You can influence the result with your belief. Belief is hugely empowering. It is the magic ingredient that can make your life extraordinary. Invest in belief.

Exercise: List out all the things that you expect to go wrong. Why do you believe they would go wrong? Is it possible for you to believe they could go right? Now hold onto your belief that things will go right no matter what happens. Make a note of how things change with belief. You will experience what you believe.

Or look at it from a reverse perspective. Your experiences reflect your beliefs. You can change your beliefs to right your experiences.

29 | TARGETS

"Man's reach should exceed his grasp, or what's a heaven for." – Robert Browning

Set targets that stretch your limits.

A CLEARLY DEFINED TARGET CREATES that mental space and prepares one to walk that path. Brian Lara's batting records include the highest score in a Test inning, a staggering 400 not out in a Test match against England at Antigua in 2004, and the record for the highest score, a mindboggling 501 not out in a first-class match for Warwickshire against Durham in 1994. Lara held the previous highest Test score of 375 against England in 1994, which was broken by Mathew Hayden of Australia, who scored 380 against Zimbabwe in 2003. Brian Lara returned with his record-breaking 400 not out within six months, in a do-or-die game for the West Indies, and raised the bar again.

Similarly, Sachin Tendulkar's incredible century of centuries in International cricket with a staggering 51 test centuries and 49 ODI centuries, combined with his being the highest run getter in both forms, stands way above all. Just as Don Bradman's seemingly unattainable average of 99.94 in 52 tests appears far beyond the reach of mortals. Champions are not easily satisfied. They push limits all the time. They aim to be the best even when they already are the best.

Every time I made up my mind to achieve a clear target, I normally succeeded. A preset target like scoring a 100 or taking a five-wicket haul will organize and stretch your efforts. Needless to say, these targets should only help you perform better and help your team win. It should not come in the way of your team's success. If you get a 100, why not a 200? A 300? Push limits all the time. I wonder how many young batsmen are setting themselves a target of breaking Lara's record of 501 not out this coming season.

I remember telling a friend on the evening prior to an inter-collegiate match in 1987 that I would score a 100 and get a five-wicket haul to get our team through the first game. I got 168 runs and five wickets in that match. Challenging myself with clear targets helped. I did not set any target for the next match. I was out for zero and got three wickets. I wonder why I did not go for 200 and seven wickets! I can fill up the page with such instances when I said I would achieve a target and did, but why did I not do it more often, like every day? For some reason, we forget the power of our thought, our intent and attribute our success to luck.

Coach's Corner

Set clear, measurable and achievable targets. Once you achieve the first target, set the next target. Targets stretch your limits. Don't be easily satisfied. Improve on your past performances with bigger targets. Your growth is as unlimited as your imagination. Challenge yourself in every job. Once it gets personal, things gets interesting.

No Ball

Having no plan and no target. Taking whatever comes. Low motivation. Afraid to take up new challenges.

In 1852, Mount Everest was officially declared the highest mountain peak at 8848 m. From 1921, expeditions began to conquer the seemingly unsurmountable Mount Everest. In 1924, the ill-fated expedition involving the disappearance of George Mallory and his partner Irvine left us mystified as to whether the peak had been scaled by them. Mallory's body was found years later. Mount Everest continued to remain a distant target for the world until Sir Edmund Hillary and Tenzing Norgay scaled the summit on May 29, 1953 as a part of the 9th British Expedition to Everest led by John Hunt. Having stretched limits and conquered the unsurmountable, Hillary and Norgay paved the way for thousands of others who scaled the peak. (As of March 2012, the Everest had been scaled 5656 times.)

My business target was pegged at a paltry ₹10 crore. I decided to challenge myself and set myself a target of ₹50 crore. I did not tell anyone about my ambitious revision as it was my own personal challenge. Every day, after work, I met prospects, collected information, analyzed it and prepared draft notes, all in my own time. By the end of the year, I had closed solid deals worth ₹80 crore. Satisfying? You bet. Did it matter if anyone was cheering me on? Not really. Knowing that I can do it if I want to was better than any applause.

Bonus Runs

When you set your own targets, you involve yourself in the process. You take ownership. You discover the route to achieve your potential and better yourself every day. You push your limits every day.

Exercise: Pick the area you want to improve your performance in. Set yourself a clear target that stretches your limits (should be attainable). Write down measurable units and the time to achieve it in. Get going. Review every week and set new targets. You will become a bigger, better person for that.

---

30 | DISCIPLINE

"Discipline is the bridge between goals and accomplishment."
– Jim Rohn

Discipline comes first to the ground.

IF ANYONE THINKS THAT GREATNESS is achieved without discipline, it's time to get the facts right. Discipline helps us do the right things in the right way and ensures consistent performances. All great cricketers acknowledge the importance of discipline in their success. Rarely do we find greats in the game being scruffy, late and unorganized. From clothes to equipment, the way they walk to the way they conduct themselves, they reflect discipline. They have a work ethic that they never break, are always before time and do things in an orderly manner. Discipline imbibes a self-restraint, an organization of thought and prepares them for the battle at hand.

We learnt much about discipline from Bro. KM Joseph at All
Saints High School. No mean cricketer himself, Bro. Joseph's
guiding hand turned talented players into better ones as he
taught discipline and values through his thoughts, words and
deeds. Punishing the mercurial Shahid Akbar for indiscipline
by making him face a wall in the corner of the ground for
an entire training session; dropping the charismatic captain
Milton Balm for coming 15 minutes late; dropping a player
who was 15 days older than the prescribed date for a prestigious
inter-school tournament; showing no discrimination between
poor or rich, race and community and only discriminating in
favour of cricketing merit, Bro. Joseph showed many young
cricketers what cricket was all about. Of course, these traditions
percolated down to us. The more disciplined ones from our
school made it to play international cricket – Azharuddin,
Venkatapathy Raju and Noel David played for India and
countless numbers played for Hyderabad.

My friend Venkatapathy Raju would always report to the
ground at six in the morning, come rain or shine. It is a feature
of his schoolboy training that every one of us remembers. His
body clock would automatically get him going, even if there
had been some major celebrations the previous night, or a long,
tiresome tour. Whatever happened, Raju was at the ground
at the prescribed hour, working away at the game. The rest
of us did not even have half his discipline. No wonder Raju
went on to play for India and performed creditably.

Coach's Corner

To perform consistently well, inculcate a disciplined work ethic; no excuses and no shortcuts. Discipline ensures that work is done, bit by bit, in an orderly fashion. Deal with the priorities first. Once the mind and body are in tune, results will show.

No Ball

Compromising attitude. Believing that mere talent will help. Excuses. Blame. Cutting corners. Unorganized approach.

I read an interview by author Frederick Forsyth, where he said that he writes from six in the morning to noon every day. Author Haruki Murakami says he gets up at four in the morning and writes for 5–6 hours a day, while writing a novel, goes for a long run or swim, listens to music, sleeps by nine – a routine which he believes enables him to mesmerize himself to reach a deeper state of the mind. Despite being seen as creative, writers and artists display tremendous discipline when it comes to their work.

Discipline set in automatically whenever I took ownership for a job. Whether it was adding the top 20 companies to our bank's client list, or scoring 128 runs for my team or writing my first book, the moment I committed myself to achieving my goal at any cost, discipline set in. Left with no escape route, my mind organized itself in the most efficient and disciplined manner to achieve the goal. Working at the most productive hours, finding ways to show up early, following set routines and pushing myself to cover every possibility within a limited time, all automatically fell into place as it was the only way to achieve those results. If it had not been for the discipline, I would not have achieved my goals.

Bonus Runs

Discipline organizes effort and makes it more efficient and purposeful. Progress is guaranteed.

Exercise: Write down a key area that could do better with a disciplined effort in your life. Commit to a disciplined effort. Put it first on the agenda every day. Start the practice even if it is just for five minutes every day, but don't miss it. You will soon find it in you to take up bigger responsibilities.

---

31 | EARNESTNESS

"To practice five things under all circumstances constitutes perfect virtue; these five are gravity, generosity of soul, sincerity, earnestness, and kindness." – Confucius.

Never be late.

PLAYING GOOD CRICKET is about being early. To take catches safely, fielders get under the ball and position themselves early to catch the ball comfortably. Batsmen get into position early to face the delivery better. In fact, batsmen who play the ball late do so, because they judge the ball early and are in position early. Bowlers decide early where to bowl. All successful players watch the ball a little earlier and prepare quicker than the rest. Teams come to ground early to prepare themselves for the match ahead. Getting into the act early gives more time to prepare, to judge and to adjust accordingly.

'Never be late' is the mantra for successful cricketers. Noel David, former Indian cricketer, recalls how Sachin Tendulkar was almost always the first in the team bus and fastidiously early for his appointments, something which is not hard to believe.

Our rector at All Saints High School, Hyderabad, Bro. KM Joseph, recounts how Mohammad Azharuddin, former Indian cricket captain, epitomized all the virtues of a good cricketer in his school days. Ten-year-old Azhar would turn up immaculately dressed in perfect whites for practice, never missed a day's practice and spent longer hours than the rest. He was always the first to report, five minutes before everyone else. You know that such earnestness will not go unrewarded. It's no wonder that Azhar achieved great heights after those early years.

Coach's Corner

Show up early. Show eagerness and earnestness as it gives you a clear edge. Anticipate and act quickly. Any delay or hesitation, and the opportunity could well disappear. Being early puts you in a better frame of mind, makes you better prepared and creates a good impression. It's good preparation. Make it a habit.

No Ball

Casual behaviour. Taking things for granted. Coming late out of fear. Disrespecting the process, people and time.

In Nagesh Kukunoor's iconic movie *Iqbal* (2005), Shreyas Talpade, who plays the lead role, is waiting at the ground for his coach, the alcoholic ex-cricketer Mohit (Naseeruddin Shah). Iqbal and his sister Khadija (Shweta Prasad) have come to the ground early, prepared it and are waiting for the coach to show up for his first lessons. When the coach does not show up, Iqbal goes in search of him and finds his coach lying in a stupor, wakes him up and coaxes him to come to the ground. No surprises that Iqbal achieves his goal with his earnest approach. When desire is high, one is never late. One shows up early.

I remember two interviews that I attended. I went late for the first interview with the arrogance of being the best in class and could not answer basic questions confidently. My lack of preparation showed and I was rightly sent off for further training by a visibly irritated interview panel. In the second interview, I went one day early, gathered information and prepared until the last minute. That interview was a breeze.

I could even answer one key question thanks to that extra bit of preparation outside the interview room. Going late will set you back and you won't do justice even to what you can normally do.

Bonus Runs

When you go early, you prepare better. You get advantages that you may miss when you go late. You get better results.

Exercise: Make it a practice to go ten minutes early everywhere. Observe how much it helps in terms of being in a better state of mind and getting information. It shows in the results too.

---

32 | PLANNING

"In preparing for battle I have always found that plans are useless, but planning is indispensable."
– Dwight D. Eisenhower

Plan your innings.

NOTHING BIG HAS BEEN ACHIEVED consistently without meticulous planning. Planning helps to visualize the future in detail, so that unforeseen glitches are prepared for. Sunil Gavsakar, Sachin Tendulkar and Rahul Dravid were models when it came to planning their innings. They played themselves in, understood the conditions and the situation, and went about crafting their innings after getting their eye in. For that matter, any batsman who has scored many hundreds at the highest level has applied this strategy. Similarly, bowlers plan their tactics to different batsmen. Captains plan their strategy well in advance. The one who has planned better, ends up being one step ahead. Much of cricket is about planning, which is why the above mentioned are more successful than others.

As Coach of the Hyderabad Ranji team, Vijay Paul would tell us the need to bat session to session, how to get away from the batting crease with a single, how to rotate strike and unsettle the bowler's concentration, how to identify times when fatigue sets in and how to overcome it by breaking the rhythm and how to plan and survive long. I never realized how much thought went into planning an inning. Vijay Paul should know, he has constructed many wonderful innings for Hyderabad.

The first time I planned on scoring a 100 was when I realized how important planning was to any project. Having a clear target in mind, I needed a foolproof way to get there. From equipment to analysis of the game, opponent strengths and weaknesses to contingent plans, all details were addressed in my head. Once I looked at all details, organized them in my mind, I got my plan in place. All I did after that was execute it. It was a wonderful feeling to get that 100.

Coach's Corner

Planning prepares you to address and overcome obstacles to your goals. If you have a detailed action plan, the probability of achieving your goals increases that much more, because all possibilities have been planned for. Visualize the plan. Write it down. Pay attention to the uncertain areas. Ask uncomfortable questions. Plan for all contingencies. The more detailed your planning, the less the uncertainty.

No Ball

Vagueness. Lazy planning. Lack of clarity. Superficial planning.

Hollywood director Woody Allen says he rarely watches his movies once they are made. He has already seen them in his head. Woody should know; he has written, directed and acted in over 60 movies and continues to do so. Movie directors, big and small, are aware that every scene they propose to shoot must be planned out in detail, in words and in images. Once they have seen their plan unfold in their mind, all they do is go ahead and implement it. Young film director and actor Srinivasa Avasarala points out that another important aspect of a director's job is to plan for unforeseen changes, so work does not suffer. Good directors normally have a plan B and plan C ready when unforeseen changes occur.

While working in the bank, I had the opportunity to analyze why certain entrepreneurs were successful and why others were not. The one big difference was their planning. The successful ones built upon their ideas and planned it all out down to the last detail. Every question was answered and all possible contingencies thought of and planned for. In fact, so well planned were they, that they had alternate plans for bank loans and were halfway into their project, whether anyone sanctioned them the loan or not. The unsuccessful ones came with a vague plan that was full of holes and full of unanswered questions. Nothing was tied up and the project could be abandoned at any moment. They hoped that things would fall into place if they bribe officials, gods, etc. for loans. Naturally, their projects never took off and we never saw that money again. No points for guessing, the former lot was the more successful.

I had a theory that I could make an 80 million issue (of bonds and improve on the previous best of 20 million), but my plan was not yet on firm ground. I needed more information to be certain. I pulled out all the data I could from the past 13 bond issues, analyzed it thoroughly and armed myself with information regarding the retail segment, large investors, wholesale segment, agents, trends, competition and associates. I made a map of the region and mapped the past investment record, district-wise, segment-wise and agent-wise. With all the information now before me, the gaps showed up and my plan fell in place. I looked at how I could tap each segment best. I contacted investors, agents, retail and wholesale customers *early. My estimate was that I could reach 80 million if I achieved about 30 percent penetration. I ended up with 160 million. I can only put that success down to planning.*

Bonus Runs

Planning improves success ratios. It reduces uncertainty and costs.

Exercise: Write down three things you want to achieve the most and the ones that are not happening. Make a one-page plan with the broad steps, possible setbacks and how to handle those setbacks. Now look at all the steps and mark the ones that you are clear and confident about. Then look at all areas that appear grey. Revisit these and get more details. These are the areas where you will slip up mostly. Once the plan feels complete, act on it. Your planning will help you achieve your goals.

---

33 | PREPARATION

"Preparation isn't about hoping for the best; it's about having a strategy to cope with the worst, whatever that takes." – from Tom Phillips book on Machiavelli's principles

Your performances reflect your preparation.

THERE IS NO LUCK, only preparation. Successful cricketers are consistent, because they prepare harder. When they are not performing, they know there's a shortfall in their preparation. Good preparation is not about hoping, it is ensuring that you get it right. Great cricketers put in detailed, specific hours preparing for oppositions, tricky pitches and unpredictable conditions until they are ready.

Preparation includes preparing on skill, physical and mental aspects over a period of time. Skill and physical fitness are addressed with methodical and proper training.

Mental preparation includes knowing the context, process and understanding one's mindset. It involves mental training, visualizing, analysis, discussion and exploration to gain greater clarity. Mental preparation helps in application of skill. It helps overcome negative patterns that limit performance.

Good preparation makes one ready and throws up opportunities. When Sachin Tendulkar made his debut for India in 1989 against Pakistan at the age of 16, there was no doubt that he was well prepared for the next level. His run of scores in the years that preceded his Test call reflects the number of hours he put in at nets and matches. His readiness was evident in the way he toyed with the bowlers at the highest level.

In their book *The Winning Way*, Anita and Harsha Bhogle recall how Sachin prepared to counter Aussie leg spinner Shane Warne in the Australia-India series in 1998. Playing the tour opener for Mumbai, Sachin scored an unbeaten double century. Shane Warne conceded 111 runs in 16 overs and went wicketless as Mumbai piled on 410 for 4. Mumbai beat Australia in three days and dented the Aussie confidence badly. But Sachin noticed that Warne didn't bowl around the wicket even once. He went four days in advance to the next Test venue and practiced playing leg spinners bowling from that angle, working on various scenarios with India's former leg spinning great

L Sivaramakrishnan, hour after hour until he got it right. Australia lost the series.

I promised my skipper that I'd score the 128 runs I'd given away while bowling. I headed straight home from the dressing room. No chai and banter at the Arts College canteen, I needed to prepare. I never made a century before, forget 128. At home, I shut myself in my room and outlined my strategy carefully. I had to bat through the 90 overs. I needed to survive the new ball, reduce errors I commonly make, deal with exhaustion and the loss of concentration. I identified and cut out risks – no cross bat shots, no cuts, no pulls, no sweeps, no flicks and glances, no improvizations for singles, no foolish calls for run outs, no airy shots and no playing away from the body. I visualized myself playing according to my plan and played those visuals over and over in my mind till midnight. Mental aspect taken care of, the preparation continued on the physical aspect next morning. I wore the most comfortable pair of whites I had, wore a cap (never wore one before, but I had 90 overs to play, you see). At the ground, I carefully chose the most comfortable pads, gloves and bat for my long sojourn at the crease. I warmed up, sat in my corner and refocused on all I prepared for the day before. I played 66 overs and scored 158. We won. A bowler who normally bats at Number eight getting 158? Attribute it to 100 percent preparation. Once I got the mindset right,

I could use my existing skill and physical aspects to turn in a match-winning performance.

Coach's Corner

The only way to perform well is to be fully prepared for every job. Put in hours to develop skills and leave nothing to chance. As your preparation gets better, appropriate opportunities will present themselves. The kind of opportunities that open up indicate your level of preparation.

No Ball

Insufficient preparation. Hoping. Excuses. Blaming bad luck. There's no such thing as bad luck, only insufficient preparation.

Malcolm Gladwell in his book *The Outliers* mentions the 10,000 hour rule (based on a study by Anders Ericsson) about how achieving greatness in any field requires 10,000 hours of practice. He cites examples of the Beatles and Bill Gates as a case in point. The Beatles played 1,200 times in the period between 1961 and 1964 in Hamburg, meeting the 10,000 hour rule. Gates had access to a high school computer in 1968 when he was 13, and worked on it for hours and hours, thereby meeting the 10,000 hour rule as well. Think young Sachin would have met the 10,000 hour rule as he criss-crossed the wickets at Shivaji Park between nets and matches for Coach Achrekar's teams?

Bonus Runs

There is no luck. There is only preparation. When you invest in preparation, you are on the growth path.

Exercise: Analyze your performances. If your performances are not upto expectation, look where your preparation is lacking – skill, physical or mental areas. Prepare on the missing aspects harder.

List out the areas that are important to your job. Look at the areas where you are not confident. Write down specific actions and metrics to prepare better in those areas. Work on it until you achieve the metrics you desire. Analyze your performance confidence now after these areas have been addressed. You will find a positive difference in the results.

---

34 | PRACTICE

"Practice does not make perfect. Only perfect practice makes perfect." – Vince Lombardi

Practice right and you get the right results.

IF YOU THOUGHT PRACTICING HARD was tough enough, here's the killer – it's not enough. The process of high performance preparation involves practicing not only hard, but more importantly, practicing right. From drills to technique, from work ethic to routines, it is about practicing correctly to gain an edge over others. Shot selection, controlling no balls and wide balls, bowling in the right areas, taking catches and running well between wickets are all important parts of a cricketer's training that come from long hours of practicing right.

To get it right, cricketers with a growth-oriented attitude do not shy away and get expert help from seniors, experts and coaches. Dean Jones is on record saying how he met Lindsay Hassett and Ian Chappell, flying at his own expense to meet them, before the Indian tour of 1986 to understand how to play spinners on Indian conditions. Indian cricketer Sunil Joshi related how he flew down to Delhi to spend time with the great left arm spinner Bishen Bedi to learn the finer nuances of left-arm spin bowling. I have witnessed the growth-oriented attitude of Rahul Dravid and Robin Uthappa among others, who sought out a coach in cricketing oblivion in Hyderabad, Mr MR Baig, to train with him for a few days off season. These are all signs of true seekers.

It is a fact that few players understand their game well enough to self-correct. Most players, even those who have played at higher levels, cannot self-correct. They feel ashamed to admit that they need to seek help, which is why a large number of players fall off the map early. There is no shame in accepting that something is going wrong and one needs help. Ask, correct and practice right.

Looking back, the times that I performed well at the game were those when I had good coaches or better cricketers around me who could correct flaws that crept into my technique. In clear contrast, when I did not have access to good coaches or helpful seniors, my game fell apart and my performances were poor. Basic mistakes went undetected and fatal errors crept into my technique. How much ever I practiced with the wrong technique was of no avail. In fact, it set me further back. I regret now not using all the opportunities when I met the experts to ask them about the craft, attitude and the intricacies.

The leg cutter, which I learnt from Dennis Lillee's book The Art of Fast Bowling, *and the yorker, which was taught to me by Shivlal Yadav in 1986, got me several wickets. I knew how to bowl those two deliveries, but I never practiced them to perfection. However, once I started using those two deliveries after practicing them well at nets, I got a lot of wickets. But hey, this was in 2002, 15 years after my playing days! Why I never practiced those two deliveries earlier in my career is a question I cannot answer. You need a growth-oriented approach and lots of practice to get into the highest levels – something that the Karnataka players Rahul Dravid, Sunil Joshi and Robin Uthappa showed. It is no surprise that Karnataka is a champion side.*

Coach's Corner

What you practice becomes your habit. Good performances result from purposeful hours spent practicing the right way; it's never about luck or talent. Luck does not favour those who practice wrong things for several hours; it is a recipe for disaster. Practice right and practice long. If you're performing well, your practice is on track. But if you're not, then get help immediately. It's not luck, it's the process. When you practice right, your performances will be effortless.

No Ball

Inconsistent performances. Blaming luck. No growth orientation. Not analyzing failures honestly and fixing what is missing.

Milkha Singh, the Flying Sikh, recalls an incident when he asked Dhyan Chand, the hockey legend who scored 400 international goals in his lifetime, how he was so good at what he did. Dhyan Chand told Milkha that he practiced hitting shots through an empty tire hung to the goal post hundreds of times every day. Dhyan Chand was named Chand (his real name was Dhyan Singh), because he would practice under the moonlight after the moon arose, as he had no time to practice during the day.

In Hyderabad, we have seen Mohammad Azharuddin taking hundreds of catches by himself after practice and VVS Laxman batting for hours at a stretch at nets and hitting more balls than most of the younger players. Legendary basketball star Michael Jordan, famous for his jump shots was initially not very good at them. He took hundreds of jump shots a day until it was perfect.

No wonder they were all so good at what they did. They did not depend on luck, they honed their skill by hours and hours of practice. How many aspirants follow their work ethic?

Invited to speak at a school in Pune, I was sipping tea with the principal and the staff after the session. One of the teachers said, "Sir, our students, they work as hard as the others. But they are not lucky. They do not get the same marks as other school children." Now wait a minute! Where does luck come into the picture? If they are studying and practicing the right things, their performance should improve. If they are not showing signs of improvement, they are probably making the same mistakes and practicing them. They need to practice right.

Bonus Runs

Perfect practice makes execution effortless.

Exercise: List all the skills you need to gain expertise in. The skills that are your bread and butter. Find the right coach. Then practice with purpose and understanding until the skill becomes second nature. Your performances will improve.

---

35 | TEAM SPIRIT

"Talent wins games, but teamwork and intelligence wins championships." – Michael Jordan

The team is always bigger than the individual.

MANY OF US HAVE FACED this dilemma – should I play for the team or should I play for myself? Most of us have realized, sometimes a bit too late, that what we had known deep in our heart was the right answer. Indian cricket's biggest moments are its World Cup victories. Images of a beaming Kapil Dev cradling the Cup at Lords in 1983, a long-haired Dhoni and his team of relative unknowns with the T20 World Cup in South Africa in 2007 and the emotional victory lap of a star-studded Indian ODI team around a charged stadium in Mumbai in 2011 flood our minds. These are victories that tower over the personal achievements of our greatest players. Even Sunil

Gavaskar's and Sachin Tendulkar's impressive resumes would have been incomplete without the World Cup wins in them. The verdict: you win only when the team wins.

Champion sides believe that the team is greater than any individual. Their passion comes from the pride each individual carries as a member of that team. In international matches, we see passionate players kissing the emblem on their caps. The Aussies take great pride in their baggy green caps. It is part of cricketing folklore in India that all Mumbai players value and take great pride in their Mumbai cap. It's not about the individual anymore, it's about the team. Get this angle in and half the battle is won already. Pride pushes people and teams to new limits. Special routines, symbols, gestures, flags, anthems, songs and visuals all evoke pride in the team.

Being part of my team – school, college, university and state, has always been a matter of immense pride and honour for me and pushed me to new limits. I bowled through the pain barrier for my junior college in a key game and got four wickets despite a back injury that caused excruciating pain. I bowled 21 overs flat out on the trot for Hyderabad in a crunch situation in a game that we finally won. I bowled for Hyderabad with a nail sticking up through the sole that made a hole in my foot by the time my spell with the new ball was completed. I bowled for my university with a torn hamstring, for my club with a fractured finger and padded up to bat with a broken nose. In each of these circumstances, it was always the pride of playing for the team that pushed me through the pain, the exhaustion and the fatigue. Some of my most prized possessions today are the caps I earned from the state team, the varsity team and my club team.

Important match. The opposition had a good batting side. The wicket had a big slope. We needed to use that advantage best as we had two decent medium pacers – Ravi and me. Though I could have gone for personal glory and helped my cause a bit by bowling down the slope and snaring more wickets as the senior bowler, I was aware that we needed to keep pressure from both ends. If the bulky Ravi found it difficult to handle the slope, we were in trouble. I gave Ravi the new ball from the top end and took the harder end, bowling up the hill. It paid off as I got three wickets and Ravi got seven. More importantly, we won the game, which is what it was all about.

Coach's Corner

The team comes first. Sign up now. Participate wholeheartedly and help your team's progress. Give 100 percent without expecting anything in return. Even if you are a lowly employee or a reserve, take your team's progress personally and help your team win. Your own good will come about in ways that you cannot imagine when your team wins. You get more opportunities at the bigger stages.

No Ball

Holding back effort consciously. Having a bargaining mindset. Selfishness. No pride. No involvement. Low commitment.

Bhagat Singh was a mere 12-year-old when he started participating in the non-cooperation movement. He knew the principle well and decided to pitch in his entire might behind his team, India. Bhagat Singh ran away from home, because his family was planning to get him married – an event that would come in the way of his cause, the freedom of his country. The young writer, thinker and rebel along with his associates launched headlong into the freedom movement, bringing their own brand of ideologies to fight the British. Bhagat Singh was hanged by the British at a tender age of 23, having lived a life that inspired millions of young Indians to fight for freedom. All that he did in his life, until his untimely death, was for his team's greater cause. No wonder the young martyr is remembered with deep appreciation and fondness by the country as Shaheed Bhagat Singh.

I was a member of the business development team for our bank. The times were exciting and opportunity great. Markets had opened up and the economy looked bullish. Instead of recognizing the opportunity and working for our team's success, we pushed papers and did an average job. We also complained about work, low pay and no recognition. One fine day, the management disbanded our team and a golden opportunity to create a mark was lost. In the next assignment, of a much smaller profile, I began working in Hyderabad with the team's interest in mind (ignoring the complaining elements in the team this time). I set myself steep targets – I achieved 800 million as against the 100 million target. As I exceeded my targets, quantitatively and qualitatively, not only did our team win accolades and our organization reap benefits, but my work got recognized and rewarded. Funnily, all that mattered then was that my team won.

Bonus Runs

When you play for your team, your commitment soars. Your performances get much better. You will be a part of a winning team. You will carry the pride of belonging.

Exercise: Write down your own personal vision for all the teams you are part of. List all the things you can do to help your team progress. Ask yourself – what more can I do for my team? Do all you can to help your team progress. Your personal growth will accelerate as your team flourishes. Find symbols that show that you are proud of being part of the team. Find ways to declare it openly, to wear your pride on your chest.

---

36 | PURPOSE

"He who has a why to live for can bear almost anyhow."
– Nietzsche

Teams are bound by a clear purpose.

SHOULD A BUNCH OF HIGH PERFORMANCe individuals be told what their purpose is before a tournament? Most of us seem to think that they ought to know. But what if each individual assumes different things, because the purpose has not been specified? Before the 2003 World Cup began, Steve Tikolo, captain of the lowly ranked Kenyan team dropped a bomb. He announced that the Kenyan team was there to win the World Cup. Many stronger teams did not have the gall to make such a bold statement. Most said that they came to play good cricket. Not surprisingly, Kenya made it to the semifinals, riding on a committed effort from its relatively unknown team. I believe that it was their clearly stated common purpose that gave the Kenyan team discipline, direction and momentum. If you have a purpose, then state it. Your team will back it.

I understood the importance of setting the common purpose clearly from Shivlal Yadav, captain of the first senior state team for Hyderabad that I played in. "We are here to play as a team and win," he declared, "and I want the best effort from everyone." That statement made the team purpose clear to all young cricketers like me, who were trying to find their way in senior cricket. Until then, we were part of teams where nothing was stated and everything was assumed. Now, with a clear purpose guiding us, we put in a spirited effort and made it to the semifinals of the Buchi Babu tournament that year, losing honourably by the spin of coin against a strong Nirlons team led by Sandeep Patil. All credit to Shiv that we pushed the mighty Nirlons to the ropes before time ran out.

For years, we were a band of players who played club cricket for fun, drank a beer and went home. The result did not matter. Why should it? We were a mixed bunch with different motives – some for fun, some for exercise, some old, some young, some with ambition and some for relaxation. But the day we said the magic word and set ourselves a common purpose of winning the league championship, everything changed. We had to let a couple of players who resented the new responsibility go, but the team came together eventually.

The result – we won that year after many, many years of playing the league.

Coach's Corner

The common purpose binds the team together. It challenges the entire team and lifts it to a higher plane. Team energies come together to fulfill the purpose. It gives a sense of worth, of togetherness. A team with a clear purpose turns up like a well-trained army as one unit and performs better.

No Ball

No common purpose. Having different or conflicting purposes. Assuming that everyone knows the common purpose. Not having everyone signed on.

In the *Mahabharata*, the armies of the Pandavas and the Kauravas aligned on the basis of their purpose. The Pandava forces rallied in support of what they believed was the right cause and fought for that one cause together. However, the vastly stronger Kaurava forces had mixed purposes for fighting the war – some for loyalty, some for friendship, some as professionals and some who had been tricked into fighting for them. As a result of their conflicting purposes, the mighty Kauravas never fought at full strength. The great warrior Karna did not enter the war as long as Bheeshma led the forces and charioteer Shalya actively worked against his own commander Karna and caused his death. So many cross purposes disrupted team unity and caused the stronger Kaurava armies to capitulate to the Pandava armies that had one common purpose – to defend the right cause.

We were not the most cohesive of teams, but our boss's wicked taunt that we were not good enough to achieve even half the target stung us. That taunt became the subject of discussion at the lunch table, at tea breaks and served to bind us all together. We vowed to achieve 50 percent higher and show him. We planned, worked long days and late nights. The result – we achieved 200 percent of the target. Our common purpose got us to work towards one direction. Many times, defeating a common enemy becomes a worthy purpose.

Bonus Runs

When everyone looks in one direction, efficiency improves that much more. Everyone is clear about the purpose and can align themselves accordingly.

Exercise: Ask your team what its common purpose is? If there is none, find it, communicate it and get the team to sign in. Ask them how they plan to achieve it, what each one will do to achieve it. You will find greater involvement from the team once the purpose is articulated.

37 | ATTITUDE

"I play to win, whether during practice or a real game. And I will not let anything get in the way of me and my competitive enthusiasm to win." – Michael Jordan

Play to win.

IT'S SURPRISING HOW MANY DIFFERENT answers you find to this question in a team – why are you playing? The answer lies in the attitudes we carry into the game. The right question, perhaps, is this – are we playing to win or hoping to win? Ian Chappell, in an article that he wrote on captaincy, mentions that captains must play to win and not be afraid of losing; this is the difference between 'playing to win' and 'hoping to win'. Teams that play to win, take risks, make sporting declarations and do not play defensive cricket. Saurav Ganguly brought the attitude of playing to win to Indian cricket in a big way – his team looked to win. Similarly, the Indian team that won the 2011 World Cup displayed an intense desire to win in the way it played, batted and fielded. Vijay Mohan Raj, who played for Ranji Trophy winning teams Bombay and Hyderabad as a batsman, recalls how there was nothing like 'doing well' in the Bombay dressing room. Their only reason to play was to win. To win, they'd compete hard, be aggressive and push one another to give their best. Playing to win is the mindset of a winner. It makes individuals and teams competitive. It aligns them fully with their purpose.

In a six-a-side tournament, our team McDowell's XI was tied with the Secunderabad Club team on runs. The match was to be decided on a shootout – the cricketing equivalent of football penalties. All bowlers had to bowl one ball at an unguarded wicket. Whichever side hits more number of times, wins. Nine bowlers out of ten from both sides bowled alternately. Amazingly, all nine missed. I was the tenth. If I hit it, we win. If I miss, all ten bowl again.

It suddenly struck me that all nine had been under pressure. Perhaps, they bowled with the thought that they should not miss – the same feeling that goes through soccer players before a penalty – bowling not to miss, instead of bowling to hit. It presented me with a golden opportunity. I had the lowest stakes to lose for the highest return. I started thinking only in terms of hitting. I cut my pace, focused on pitching the ball full and hit the middle and off stumps. We won 1–0. There's a difference between shooting to hit and shooting not to miss.

Coach's Corner

To win, be honest and clear that you want to win. Make your intention clear. It will give you the competitive edge. You will win more than you lose with that attitude. Do not be afraid to lose. When you fear losing, you become defensive. Commit yourself fully to the purpose.

No Ball

Being clear about what you 'don't want'. Hoping others will understand what you want and give it to you. Giving up in the big moments. Not preparing for big moments.

In the famous book *The Secret* by Rhonda Byrne, experts talk about how thoughts are creative and about the law of attraction. Giving attention to 'not losing' repeatedly brings the word 'losing' into play, and that is what eventually manifests. Focus on 'winning' and it will manifest that result. An interesting thought, because it sets the ground for a clear mindset. Whatever it is, be clear about what you want.

In World War II, Great Britain was clear that it would fight on till victory was achieved against Germany despite having almost nothing in reserve. The attitude that British Prime Minister Winston Churchill brought to the war gave British troops and civilians rare hope. They fought against superior air power and daringly held back the German assault with meager reserves. The British attitude was clear – victory at all costs. It was not to put up a good show. They won against all odds.

I remember two campaigns in a marketing assignment: One, where we worked with the mindset that we would hope for the best; the second, where we said that we would achieve our targets at all costs. When we 'hoped', we had no target, no process, no accountability, no monitoring and consequently, no performance. None of us grew as people, there was low self-esteem and low team involvement. The result – out of an expected target of ₹80 million, we achieved only ₹20 million. On the other hand, when we played to win, we were clear about what we wanted to achieve, and how to achieve it. The results were excellent – we achieved ₹160 million of the original ₹80 million. Everyone grew and felt good at having been part of that campaign. The difference was just the mindsets that we approached the two campaigns with.

Bonus Runs

When you are clear about what you want to achieve, it becomes that much easier to get it. You get the winning edge.

Exercise: Pick the important aspects of your life – career, relationships, health, wealth and social life. Ask yourself what you want from them honestly. Write down what you want in clear, specific and measurable terms. Visualize the feeling of having achieved the goal. Does it excite you? Does it make you feel good enough to take complete responsibility for its achievement? Do you feel like saying, "I will achieve it, whatever happens!" Your chances improve if you go for them.

---

38 | SUPPORT

"We are all in the same boat, in a stormy sea, and we owe each other a terrible loyalty." – GK Chesterton

Backing up.

EVER THOUGHT WHY WE SUPPORT some people and pull down some others? Why we support perfect strangers and not our own family members? But we cannot afford to do that in any team game, least of all cricket. Non-strikers back their partners, ready to run a quick single for them. Fielders back up when others throw, so they can throw confidently. Cricketers back teammates on their off days; they know that everyone has an off day and needs support from the team. Backing up by crowds pumps up players, such as the famous 'Lil-lee, Lil-lee' chant across Australian grounds, which inspired the legendary Australian fast bowler Dennis Lillee to bowl even faster, much to the dismay of the opposition's batsmen. Nothing like some unconditional support to spur one to a higher effort.

In the Test series between Australia and Sri Lanka in 1995, Australian umpire Darrel Hair called Sri Lankan off-spinner Muthiah Muralitharan for throwing. The Sri Lankans felt that Muthiah's action was legitimate as it had passed muster from other umpires across the world in the 22 matches he had played till then. They contested the decision. Sri Lankan skipper Arjuna Ranatunga backed Muthiah Muralitharan to the hilt. When Murali was called in 1999 by umpire Ross Emerson, Arjuna even threatened to walk off the field with his team, bringing international cricket to a dangerous place. Although the ICC cleared Murali's action, the controversy rages on. But through all that, the unconditional support the Sri Lankan team lent to their mate is praiseworthy. Muralitharan repaid the unflinching support from his skipper and teammates, who were willing to face severe consequences for him, and garnered an astounding 800 wickets in test cricket, establishing Sri Lanka as a force to reckon with in the process. All for one and one for all.

Cricket selections were announced at school. I badly wanted to get selected and wanted to practice before the selections. It was June in Hyderabad and it was pouring buckets, but Ram, my brother, then all of 12, fully supported my endeavour and bowled manfully through heavy rain for well over an hour – a big effort for his frail frame. Our well-intentioned efforts came to naught when I came down with heavy fever (though it was Ram who bowled in the rain) and I could not go to the selections, but it warms the heart to feel supported like that. Ram continues to bowl in the rain even today, whenever I need support.

Coach's Corner

Support every endeavour you are associated with wholeheartedly. Friends and family, colleagues and neighbours, performers and youngsters, everybody wants to do well and win applause and appreciation. Back them fully. Make them feel they can and they will perform miracles. Extend support even if you don't believe in the person or the project. Support and judgment are two different things. All you have to do is choose your response. Choose in favour of support always.

No Ball

False show of support intended to demoralize you. Backbiting. Conspiracies to pull each other down. Disloyal members. Criticism that impacts performances negatively.

In the *Mahabharata*, the great warrior Karna, is prevented from participating in an important archery contest, because he is not of royal birth. He is made fun of for being the son of a charioteer. Alone in his hour of humiliation, Karna finds unexpected support from the Kaurava prince Duryodhana, who makes him the King of Anga, and allows him to participate. For this act of support, Karna remains loyal to Duryodhana and repays his support with his life, even spurning an offer to become the King of Hastinapur if he agreed to fight alongside his brothers, the Pandavas.

I had been away on unauthorized leave for four months and then, to top that, I wanted a transfer. Most bosses would have thrown me out of the room (some did), but Mr Bedekar knew of the loyalties that one can get in return when people's anxieties are understood, their aspirations supported. He gave me the transfer against all expectations and then told me his condition – he said he expected me to be one of the best officers for the bank. For the next six years, I repaid his trust with my loyalty and with my best work. Those words remained with me throughout my stay in the bank. One word, one act of support is all it takes to buy such loyalty.

Bonus Runs

When you give, you get. Your unconditional support will earn you loyal friendship that can never be bought.

Exercise: Starting this moment, support your teammates, friends, family or others wholeheartedly in whatever way you can. Write down all the ways in which you will pledge support and do it. Call them and tell them you fully support them. See how your words perk them up, how they transform from being insecure and defensive into open, giving people. Practice being supportive at every opportunity you get. Your own life will change as you help others find belief in their abilities from your words and actions.

39 | PARTNERSHIPS

"Alone we can do so little; together we can do so much." – Helen Keller

Build partnerships.

HOWEVER GREAT AN INDIVIDUAL, he is nothing without partners who complement his efforts. To acknowledge and build healthy partnerships is the only way forward for all of us who live in this interwoven, interconnected world. Cricket teams focus on partnerships to build big scores. Much thought goes into nurturing partnerships. From senior partners taking more strike initially, helping new batsmen settle down, shielding one another, giving advice, sharing information, motivating one another through tough periods and rotating strikes, teams know that partnerships are the key to big totals.

When South Africa chased down Australia's massive

score of 434 in a one day game at Johannesburg in 2006, the biggest run chase in a One Day International match till date, the score card showed partnerships at every wicket almost. From Hershelle Gibbs who scored 175 to Makhaya Ntini who scored one run, everybody contributed.

The most successful teams in cricket history relied on building partnerships. The West Indies, for example, had a batting line up that thrived on building partnerships. Gordon Greenidge, Desmond Haynes, Vivian Richards, Clive Lloyd, Alvin Kallicharran, Larry Gomes and others made life miserable for the opposition bowling sides. Fast bowlers are considered most effective when they hunt in pairs – Dennis Lillee and Jeff Thomson, Waqar Younis and Wasim Akram, Joel Garner, Andy Roberts, Michael Holding and Malcolm Marshall. When partnerships build, the opposition is under pressure.

While playing for the Hyderabad Junior team in the mid 80s, we had a good lower order (popularly called the nine, ten, Jack) batting in Rajesh Yadav, Abhijit Chatterjee, Venkatapathy Raju and me – all bowlers who could bat a bit. In a key game, we were 150 for 6 and looking at a prospect of being bowled out for a low score, but we focused on building partnerships, rotating the strike, talking to one another and added almost 150 runs between us. Our late partnerships frustrated the opposition. We came back and bowled well in tandem and

won the game later. We figured in many such partnerships
for Hyderabad for both bowling and batting. No wonder we
were part of teams that won all the junior level tournaments
for Hyderabad. Three of us: Rajesh, Venkatapathy and I
played in the year that Hyderabad won the Ranji Trophy
too, with Rajesh starring in the final against Delhi with a
five-wicket haul!

Coach's Corner

Partnerships help you achieve things that you cannot achieve by yourself. Look to build and nurture as many productive partnerships as you can. You can develop synergistic partnerships in the most unlikely places around you. Social circles, families, school and college mates, colleagues at work, neighbors, acquaintances can contribute for you in many ways if you are willing to let them. Building partnerships makes your life more meaningful, purposeful and stress-free. Look to integrate, to go win-win.

No Ball

Egoistic and isolated behaviour. Selfish players. Untrustworthy, short-term partnerships.

AMUL or Anand Milk Federation Union Limited, is an Indian dairy cooperative based at Anand in Gujarat. It is jointly owned by three million milk producers. Formed in 1946, AMUL is the reason behind India's White Revolution, a project that made India the leading producer of milk and milk products in the world. AMUL's story started from the hapless voices of exploited milk producers in Kaira, who were unhappy with the prices paid to them. The farmers partnered together across districts and unions over a period of time, creating one of the greatest brands in India. More importantly, they highlighted the power of what partnerships can do to empower people.

There is an interesting story of the partnership forged between Microsoft and Apple when Apple was struggling. Microsoft pumped in USD 150 million into Apple in 1997 with a five-year commitment. It was seen as partnering with the enemy, but both saw sense in such a partnership for different reasons – Apple needed the help and Microsoft needed competition. Both companies gained from that unlikely partnership as we can see today. If Steve Jobs and Bills Gates could partner, so could we!

Our Head Office instructed us to terminate the 550 dormant agents attached to us. We dutifully began the process. However, Kumar, our boss thought differently. He decided to activate our 'sleeping partners' instead. "How can we lose 550 partners so easily?" he countered. He made us call every single one of them with instructions to address any issues they may have and reactivate their deposit mobilization efforts. Within a fortnight, 350 agents were raising deposits in a small way. The result – our retail component jumped from 30 percent of the total to 70 percent. Our collection figure was eight times what we had achieved in the previous drive. Kumar's 350 extra partners did the trick for us. They were happy, we were happy and surely our customers were happy. How many such partnerships are we ignoring and terminating thoughtlessly?

Bonus Runs

Open, trusting, equal partners make life easy and fun. Together you can achieve much more.

Exercise: Write down all the partnerships that exist in your life. Which among those can be made stronger? Those that can be started afresh? Activate and strengthen your partners. All you may need is a hello, a smile and an open attitude to get things going. You will find that you can get more done with less effort by building partnerships.

---

40 | LEADERSHIP

"Good leadership consists of showing average people how to do the work of superior people." – John D Rockefeller

The captain holds the key.

GREAT RESULTS ARE ACHIEVED when great passions are contained and given direction and this is exactly what great leaders do. Inspirational captains like Ian Chappell, Clive Lloyd, Mike Brearley, Mansur Ali Khan Pataudi, Kapil Dev, Imran Khan, Arjuna Ranatunga, Steve Waugh, Saurav Ganguly and MS Dhoni among others have proven how invaluable a captain's role can be in shaping their team's destinies. Having a team of lions is of no use if it is led by a sheep; it is potential wasted. On the other hand, a lion can make a bunch of sheep look dangerous in battle. Leadership is not a seniority issue, it's a skill issue.

Leaders inspire, have a vision, passion and take the team to a higher level.

A raw young, inexperienced MCC was facing the champion Syndicate Bank side in 1984. The bank side was loaded with seasoned, veteran first-class cricketers and was led by a combative Test cricketer, Shivlal Yadav. We were a bunch of school and college boys led by a retired Test cricketer ML Jaisimha, renowned for his cricketing acumen. Chasing our total of 265, the bank men got off to a poor start and were 20 for 2 overnight. The noose got tighter and tighter and they were bundled out for 135 the next day. I got five of those wickets. With timely bowling changes, precise field placements and specific instructions to bowlers, Jai Uncle's captaincy was the big difference that made a bunch of us rookies perform out of our skins that day. Riding on that one upset win, many of us youngsters got recognition and opportunities to play a higher grade of cricket that year – eight of us were in the Ranji Trophy probables list.

Coach's Corner

Pick leaders who are best qualified to achieve the overall objective. They can make better people and create better futures. Leaders with vision and compassion, character and wisdom, courage and kindness, will and moral fibre can make an ordinary team achieve extraordinary results. They will unite, rise above and allow the people to do greater good for themselves. Find those leaders.

No Ball

Sentimental, parochial and short-sighted leaders hurt everyone. A bad leader can set the team back miles. Don't make emotional choices.

Living under white domination and the inhuman rules of racism and apartheid, Nelson Mandela fought for his "ideal of a democratic and free society in which everyone live together in harmony and with equal opportunities." This was an ideal for which he said he was prepared to die. Nelson Mandela spent 27 years of his life in jail chasing his ideal. He rejected three conditional offers of release, stuck to his guns and forced the world to accede to his ideal. Mandela was elected the first black President of South Africa, and led with exemplary honesty, courage, persistence, fearlessness, decisiveness, strategic vision and great wisdom. He remains one of the truly great global leaders. Leaders of such quality can change lives of nations. Find them. Prop them. Get them to office. Get the right leader in your teams to begin with.

I remember two bosses clearly. One, who took our entire team to a new level and helped everyone on board grow. Each one of us in his team got promoted, got exposure and took away great credentials. The other one never gave us space, never trusted us and never gave us any exposure. We all left with nothing to show and were short of confidence. Some talented and committed youngsters even quit the company because of him. We were all poorer for that experience. We learned from both of course – what one should do from the good boss and what one should not do from the bad boss.

Bonus Runs

Good leaders make a significant difference to the outcome and to your futures. They can change lives.

Exercise: Start thinking like the leader, irrespective of your position in the team. Chart your vision for your team. At home, at work, in the community and in society. List out the ways in which you can get your team to perform. Involve your team members in the process by helping their growth. You will find a rare energy in your work once you take a leader's attitude towards it.

---

41 | MAN-MANAGEMENT

"The conventional definition of management is getting work done through people, but real management is developing people through work." – Agha Hasan Abedi

Get the best out of your resources.

EVERYONE WANTS TO DO THEIR BEST, but how you get them to do it is the question. Cricket captains and coaches know that their job is to get the best of the resources they have. They cannot blame the resources. Blaming your resources only reflects on your leadership skills.

MS Dhoni is a successful leader, because he gets the best out of his resources on a regular basis. In the T20 World Cup in South Africa, Dhoni got a bunch of inexperienced, young players to perform and won the championship against all odds. He has been able to do this many times over the years since. He believes in his players' abilities, gives them space and responsibility and trusts them to find their way. He throws them into the deep end and lets them take ownership for their individual and the team's success. And of course, he acknowledges their effort every time. It needs a compassionate and secure person to do that.

As captain, I noticed this anomaly one season. We won all the matches that we played with our regular team (no stars), but when we got a couple of stars for an important match and were far stronger on paper, we lost the key match. I realized then that it was not about having the best resources, but about getting the best out of them. In the match, when I had the best resources, I clearly failed to lead well and get the best out of my strengthened team members. I made the mistake of expecting the stars to win the match for us, while we sat and enjoyed the show. It never works that way.

Coach's Corner

It's not about what you have, but what you do with what you have. Make your resources perform and get the results you want. Your job is to get them to contribute their best. Make things interesting for them. Challenge, involve and help them grow. Each resource is different. Understand what makes them tick. A good leader can make ordinary resources perform above their weight. Here's a clue – to get the best out of people, you have to really care for them as people.

No Ball

Expecting people to give their best by themselves, because they won't. It's your job to get the best out of them by creating the right environment.

Spartan King Leonidas led a band of 300 Spartan warriors to counter an immensely strong Persian army (almost 300,000 according to some estimates) led by Xerxes of Persia – a battle that became the subject of the Hollywood movie 300 (2006). Legend has it that while the Spartan Council was pondering over the decision of whether Sparta should go to war, King Leonidas with 300 of his best soldiers halted the mighty Persians from invading Sparta. He chose a narrow corridor at Thermopylae to engage with the Persians, a path so narrow "that numbers don't count". The brave Spartans held back the superior Persians for three days, fighting for their Sparta as a single unit, during which time the Council accorded permission for war. Leonidas and his band finally succumbed, betrayed by a local who revealed a way to outflank the brave Spartans to the Persians. This war remains among the best examples of man–management, where a few beat many. King Leonidas's statue still stands as a testimony of his leadership skills, where he made his 300 soldiers fight far above their weight, with his famous words inscribed beneath 'Come and take' in response to the Persian command to throw down their weapons. In the famous battle of Panhalgad in Maharashtra, Shivaji's general Baji Prabhu Deshpande fought with an estimated 1,000 soldiers against an estimated 15,000 enemy soldiers and helped Shivaji escape from the besieged fort. In each case, the leaders got their team to perform way above their capabilities. Situations that young MSD would identify with?

New team – one newcomer, two reluctant seniors who did not want extra responsibility and an inexperienced leader to top things. Knowing that it would be suicidal to boss the team around, I told them what was expected. I told them that they had total freedom on how to go about achieving their tasks as long as we delivered as a team. It was not all smooth sailing. There were times when I had to push, bully and cajole, but given the freedom, support and comfort, our team did a great job. We ended up putting in about four times the work and got results that surprised us more than anyone else, surpassing our targets. As the leader, I realized that I had to go an extra step to understand their anxieties, address them and make them feel as if they owned the project themselves. I was not guiding them, they did it themselves.

Bonus Runs

As a leader, your job becomes easier when others step in to take greater part. It is easiest when everyone in the team strives to achieve the goal.

Exercise: Look at the resources at your disposal. See the potential within them. Write it down. Now write down beside each one of them, ways and means to draw the potential out of them. Extract those performances from them. You will find them responding to your expectation of their potential.

---

42 | TRUST

"Never tell people how to do things. Tell them what to do
and they will surprise you with their ingenuity."
– General S Patton

Trust your intuition, yourself and your team.

TRUST PLACES A RESPONSIBILITY on people that words
cannot. To trust another fully, however, one needs to trust
oneself. In the final of the T20 World Cup in South Africa
in 2007, MS Dhoni trusted Joginder Sharma to bowl the
crucial last over. I believe that it was the implicit trust that
Dhoni showed in Sharma to deliver (even after a couple of
bad deliveries) that gave Joginder the space to recover and
cause Misbah's dismissal. Would you have done it if you
were in Dhoni's place? Would you still show your trust
and support after that wide and that six? Most would go
into the blame game and yell and cuss at the bowler for

letting their trust down. But that is what trust is all about; to trust the other person even more than he or she does, when they are at the lowest point of their confidence. To trust another, you need to trust yourself fully.

In a do-or-die match against Bangalore University, I played my last dice as skipper – the new ball. The opposition needed 45 runs with six wickets in hand. I got a wicket in my first over. The spell from the other end was critical. Against all conventional wisdom, I decided to trust the new ball with CV Anand, my pedantic young friend, who could swing the ball away in a banana curve from the batsman and generate a decent amount of nip off the surface. I said nothing; I trusted him to get us wickets and the gamble paid off – CV picked up two quick wickets and we got them down to nine wickets. Though we lost a close game, I realized that as captain, it is important to trust your intuition and your players' abilities.

It was the last game of a season of bad losses. We had lost games we should have won due to sudden collapses and silly mistakes. That game, we still needed 70 runs to win with only two wickets in hand. Something clicked in my head and I let go of the invisible control in my mind. I told the batsmen that I trusted them to do their best and they can play their game the way they want, whatever the result. And I let go. As I *walked around the ground sipping chai peacefully (instead of constantly shouting instructions and advising them), the last wicket pair added more than 50 runs and we won. I learned that day how much pressure I was putting on the boys by not trusting them to do their job. I wanted results, but did not trust them to deliver. As long as I held onto that mistrusting thought, they felt it as physically as if it were a chain. They were tied down by it. The moment I let go in my head, I gave them the space to find their own way. I learned much about trust that day.*

Coach's Corner

People give their best when they feel trusted. They go out of their way and do that extra bit for the team. Paradoxically, trust is really about getting yourself out of the way and letting the team members do their job. Tell them what you want and trust them to do it. They will find a way to deliver. To trust others, trust yourself first. Trusting does not mean abandoning them to their own devices. Let go of the string, but keep an eye on them so they have a safety net in case they fall. Tell yourself you'll handle things even if they goof up. Trust is about letting go of the need to be in control and allowing them to grow, even if they make mistakes.

No Ball

Doing everything yourself. Not allowing them to do it on their own. Blaming others. Constantly breathing down their necks. Not trusting them to do it by themselves. Not allowing them to try and fail.

I heard this true story of trust between two business partners. One of them had some legal issues in starting the business in his name. He put up his money in his friend's name with the verbal agreement that his share would be transferred back after a year's time when his issues were settled. During the one-year period, the small business grew phenomenally into a multi-million dollar business. There were doubts whether his implicit trust would be repaid. As everyone held their breath to see what drama would unfold on the day, his business partner, someone he had only known for a few months, turned up at his doorstep and returned him his entire share without a word being asked. If he had even for a second, doubted his friend, I feel it might have been a different story.

With a huge conference to be hosted for over 300 of our agents in a star hotel, I asked my young team to handle it. They told me that they had never done anything like this before and that it would be a disaster if I left it to them. But I told them I trusted them and asked them to do a great job of it to the best of their ability. It turned out that a raw team of three handled more than 300 guests (past turnouts were less than 50) on that day, hosted the event grandly and graciously, and made us all proud. I trusted them and they exceeded my expectations.

Bonus Runs

Trust brings great results. It gives back far more than you think you may lose.

Exercise: Look at all the things that bother you about others and the way they do things. Notice the ones you criticize the most. List them all down. Then, let go of each of those mentally. Trust yourself to trust them. Let them do it their way. See how well they do the job when you let go in your mind. You will find that people go to great lengths to deliver if you trust them.

---

43 | EMPOWERMENT

"The art of teaching is the art of assisting discovery." – Mark Van Doren

Get everyone to grow.

WHAT DO WE DO with the 'weak links' in the team? Most leaders crib about them, but good captains carefully nurture their growth. Only someone who genuinely loves his people would want the weakest links to grow beyond their limitations. When they do grow, they add hugely to the bottom line and take a lot of pressure off the team. When tail enders add vital runs, when fielders pull off unlikely catches and effect brilliant run outs and when change bowlers get important wickets, these seemingly small contributions add great, unexpected value to their teams. Every little extra these players contribute makes a huge difference in the end. Teams where fringe players contribute that ten percent extra win more games. On the contrary, teams that rely on one or two star players lose out on these bonuses, as everyone is looking at the stars to perform all the time. Such teams operate below their full potential.

In the 1983 World Cup, India's stars were its lesser known players. Madanlal, Roger Binny, Yashpal Sharma, Balwinder Sandhu, Kirti Azad and others chipped in with key contributions and added up to the big picture. It was they who did it for India, not the stars. For many years, Robin Singh, Ajay Jadeja and the like did this job wonderfully for India and impacted results positively.

How does one get fringe players to contribute? Empower them, give them opportunities and space to grow. Support and back them. By believing in their potential, something they have not yet seen in themselves, the leader can help them grow and make bigger players out of them.

Chasing 280 against Nizam College, my skipper Vivek Jaisimha promoted me (I normally batted at seven or eight) to open the batting, despite having many good batsmen on the side. With no pressure on myself, I went at the opposition bowling and scored a rapid 112 in 20 overs. We won the game easily with our batsmen hardly breaking a sweat, since a non-batsman like me had done the bulk of the scoring in what could have been a dicey game otherwise. By empowering a fringe batsman with greater responsibility, Vivek did our team a huge favour. He also helped me grow as a cricketer as I now qualified to open the batting for our team. I was now a hundred-man!

Coach's Corner

When everyone contributes a little extra, bottom lines soar. Identify players in your team who are under no pressure to deliver, the fringe players. Provide them with opportunities to contribute more. By giving them exposure and space, you get bigger contributions from them and your team performs much better. Good for them, fantastic for the team.

No Ball

Ignoring fringe players totally and focusing only on your star players. Not giving weak players opportunities to grow.

Empowerment of women and subjugated classes were major steps that changed the direction of the world in the last century. Abolition of slavery, equal rights to women, end of apartheid and of untouchability – humanity has realized that to move forward we need bigger contributions from the ones who have been kept on the fringe, the ones who have been excluded. Imagine our world if slavery, discrimination based on colour, sex, race, religion and caste continued to be the guiding laws to this day. Imagine how much of the good work done by these excluded classes would have been missed by the world. Now, it's time to empower more fringe partners in our environment by giving more opportunities and removing traditional barriers that restrict. Are we secure enough to do that?

The World War II created a huge requirement of jobs in the US. Men were moved to the war front, which required many minorities to be brought in to fill the gaps at manufacturing, postal, nursing and other jobs. Women, African Americans, native Americans, Mexicans and other groups were recruited in large numbers. Women were employed in factories to boost production and African Americans fought alongside white Americans and claimed an equal credit. Mexicans and Native Americans, the most famous of those being the Navajo code talkers, a group that was used to communicate in their code to confound the Japanese intercepts of American communications, were other highlights of how the fringe players played a great role and added to the bottom line when they were allowed to. We just cannot afford to keep anyone out.

When our boss suddenly quit one day before an important public issue of bonds that we were gearing up for, it was the worst thing that could have happened at that stage. Our last issue had been a disaster and our department was under pressure to perform. Against all expectations in such a delicate situation, our general manager entrusted the job to a bunch of us juniors instead of assigning it to other reluctant senior managers. With no real pressure on us and all the strength we derived from his confidence in us, we worked with a rare commitment and delivered results beyond his expectations. It was a challenge and we wanted to prove ourselves. It paid off for our boss as we achieved 150 percent of the target. Our GM had all the makings of a good cricket skipper.

Bonus Runs

When you empower everybody in the team, bottom lines soar. Team performances improve. There is less pressure on the team and more resilience within it.

Exercise: Write down all the ways in which you can help the fringe players in your team grow by about ten percent. It gives a whole new dimension to your resources when you seek to help them grow with new challenges. Ultimately, the whole team grows.

---

44 | COMMUNICATION

"The single biggest problem in communication is the illusion that it has taken place." – George Bernard Shaw

Call early, clearly, loudly.

LAST WICKET PAIR, Allan Donald and Lance Klusener, were involved in a dreadful run out that cost South Africa a place in the 1999 World Cup final. It was a tragic case of communication gone wrong. To avoid such mishaps, batsmen are trained to call when they run between wickets. They call loud and clear in a prescribed manner – yes, no, waiting – whose call, how to call and what to call. Similarly, fielders train to call for catches when they are in the best position to take the catch to reduce risk of injury and dropped catches. Lack of communication can prove costly to fielders – a collision between Australian captain

Steve Waugh and Jason Gillespie in the Test match at Kandy versus Sri Lanka in 1999 resulted in a broken nose and a broken shin, respectively. Captains continuously communicate with fielders verbally and non-verbally. Bowlers communicate with fielders and wicketkeepers. Without clear and effective communication, teams cannot work effectively.

Playing a practice match against the Zimbabwe squad in the 1988 Reliance Cup, I was in good spirits having glanced fast bowler Eddo Brandes down to fine leg for four. But I learned soon enough why Zimbabwe was one of the best fielding sides in that competition, that is, when I took off as usual without any call to my partner and was run out by miles. I never felt so foolish – the opposition was almost in a conference by the time I reached the crease.

In another instance, I remember how my poor calling cost us. My friend Chetan Joshi and I were staging a recovery act of sorts and had added 45 runs. It was looking good until I played a ball into a gap at the cover, started off and then stopped without calling. That bit of hesitation got Chetan, who trusted my initial reaction to come down. He was run out. Only later, when I was more secure as a cricketer and person, did I realize the importance of calling out loud and clear. It's something that I take into all team related activities now.

Coach's Corner

Communicate early, clearly and loudly. Ensure that everybody is on the same page. Double check to eliminate any assumptions. Say it. Write it. Get it across. Good communication avoids costly, unnecessary mistakes. Use precise language. Clarify. It makes life so much easier.

No Ball

Assuming that others would know. Negligence. Laziness. Failing to communicate. Reluctance to communicate. Lack of clarity.

In the bestselling book *The Checklist Manifesto – How to Get Things Right*, Dr Atul Gawande emphasizes the need for better communication between medical teams to get things right. Dr Gawande developed process and communication checklists to contain the four major glitches in surgery – infection, bleeding, unsafe anesthesia and the unexpected. The results of his experiments with checklists in eight hospitals across the globe were encouraging to say the least. The two minute, 19-step surgery checklist brought down major complications by

36 percent, deaths by 45 percent, infection rates by 50 percent and patients returning due to complications by 25 percent. This is a clear case of how simple communication can make things better.

On September 23, 1999 NASA lost a Mars Orbiter in space. The reason: Lockheed Martin Engineers used the English measurement system and the agency used the metric system for a key spacecraft operation. The two different systems of measurement prevented the spacecraft's navigation coordinates from being transferred from a spacecraft team in Denver to a lab in California. The Mars Orbiter was lost in space and NASA lost USD 125 million. Proper calling at the right time was all they needed to do to avoid the confusion.

In a three-day workshop that our Professors, B Trivikrama, Balaji and Hanumantha Rao, conducted for us during our MBA course at Osmania University, I learned the real essence of communication. They made us play the Chinese whisper and I was amazed at how drastically our perception could distort communication. I've made it a point ever since to ensure that me and the other person are on the same page, even at the cost of being repetitive and boring, but definitely not at the cost of not communicating.

Bonus Runs

Good communication increases efficiency, reduces costs and keeps out unpleasant surprises.

Exercise: Play the Chinese whisper with your team. Nothing like that game to get your perspective clear on the importance of communication. Also, the next time you communicate something to the team, ask them to tell you what they understood individually. It could throw up some interesting scenarios.

---

45 | JUSTICE

"To sin by silence, when they should protest, makes cowards of men." – Ella Wheeler Wilcox

Howzaat!

ASK OR YOU SHALL NOT receive. Cricketers appeal to umpires to get a verdict. If they do not appeal, the umpire is not obliged to respond. On several occasions, batsmen have continued batting because fielding sides have failed to appeal.

So important is the art of appealing, that some sides and individuals have made a fine art of it. Dennis Lillee's famous appealing style, where he would turn back in his follow through, go low on his haunches, point his finger directly, look the umpire in the eye and appeal in the most convincing of manners was a style that might well have tipped a couple of decisions in his favour. I-want-justice-

and-I-will-fight-for-it, was probably his credo. Shoaib Akhthar and Zaheer Khan are others who would appeal passionately to the umpire. These bowlers really make the umpire think hard about the judgment. Teams go up in unison and appeal loudly at the slightest doubt, advancing in anticipation and making the umpire feel the pressure of a confident appeal. Sometimes, when teams forget to appeal, umpires have the last laugh, but the process is clear – if you want a verdict, you have to ask, promptly and confidently.

My friend Vidyuth Jaisimha told me an interesting story that happened during schools cricket. Batsman Vidyuth was out by yards. Bowler Masood Ahmed (later my captain) gently touched the stumps with the ball and left it at that. The fielding team converged and started celebrating what they thought was a clear run out. Vidyuth however noticed that the bails had not been taken off, nor had Masood appealed to confirm if the batsman was given out. He sauntered back into his crease. When the perplexed opposition looked at the umpire for his verdict, he ruled Vidyuth not out because the bails had not been taken off. Now, if Masood had appealed when Vidyuth was half way down the wicket, he might have got some inkling that perhaps he needed to take the bails off. Someone could have rectified the mistake. Appeal loudly when you want something.

Coach's Corner

If you want something, ask. Never assume that you will be told, provided the information or your innermost feelings understood. It could save you much trouble later. When you ask, you could get anything. Don't assume and give up. Appeal.

No Ball

Postponing. Not asking. Assuming. Bearing injustice. Hoping someone will notice.

Inventor Robert Kearns, whose story was captured in the Hollywood film *Flash of Genius* (2008), appealed for justice against automobile majors Ford and Chrysler in one of the most famous infringement cases in history. His invention, the intermittent windshield wiper system was used by the automobile manufacturers without giving him neither credit nor payment. Kearns appealed, fought a long legal battle that cost him his marriage, USD 10 million and perhaps much of his health, but he eventually won, defending his case himself, with help from his family. Ford paid him USD 10 million and Chrysler paid an estimated USD 30 million. Most of us could gain inspiration and use this right to appeal as Kearn has done successfully.

Choudary, an industrialist friend of mine, narrates the story of how he got his license from the Ministry of Industries for the new granite factory he had planned to start, post the license Raj of 1991. Harassed by the red tape in Delhi, and seeing his hopes of securing the paper dashed almost, he forced an unannounced entry into the concerned Secretary's office on the last day, and appealed to him for help. The Secretary saw the emotional young man who had returned from Australia to India with hope, sat him down, understood the case and got the job done in an hour. Choudary had been working on that clearance for a month, following his precious file through a complex maze of consultants, commission agents, babus until he decided to appeal. He got the verdict in his favour.

Bonus Runs

You could get justice every time you appeal. Have faith in the process.

Exercise: What are all the jobs that you have left out in the back burner, because you feel you may not get any justice? Appeal to the proper authorities. Write a letter. Send an email. SMS. If they do not respond, get prepared to go to higher authorities. To the President of India. Use your rights. You will find unexpected responses if you appeal.

---

46 | HUMILITY

"Humility is not thinking less of yourself, it's thinking of yourself less." – CS Lewis

The game is bigger than the players.

THE GREATEST PLAYERS REALIZE that they are merely the medium through which the game, and life itself, expresses itself. They appreciate the opportunity they have been given. Sachin Tendulkar, Rahul Dravid and Anil Kumble among many others of their stature have always respected the game and have shown their humility and gratitude through their acts and words. Humility reflects on you as a person, your learning and how you relate to your environment.

Kicking the ball, flinging the bat, throwing down the cap, disrespecting any part of the equipment or the environment, disregarding the process, disrespecting people who made you what you are (from coaches to groundsmen) is a sure recipe for a rapid downfall. The ones who have mistakenly assumed that they are greater than the game, have without exception, paid a price for their arrogance, dishonesty and immaturity. The game lives forever, while players come and go. It goes without saying, the game is bigger than the individual.

Despite his phenomenal success, Sachin Tendulkar, often described as a God himself, carries himself impeccably. He has never had phases where he had grown arrogant and behaved as if he was above the game. He always behaved like a good student, a devoted practitioner and treated all aspects of the game that gave him so much with respect, be it his fitness, his practice regime, his commitment to the game, his colleagues and his teams. He did not speak disrespectfully of those who belittled him and let his bat do the talking always. The result of such humility shows in the success and respect he has earned. When you respect the medium, it respects you. The same goes for all the other greats mentioned and unmentioned.

In a talk that he gave to young cricketers at the ML Jaisimha Cricket Academy in Hyderabad, Kapil Dev said:

"When you have a ball in your hand as a medium pacer or as a spinner, you must treat it well. You must shine it and keep it in the best condition. You must respect it and only then will

it work for you. Shine the ball and it will work wonders for you." Wonderful advice.

Coach's Corner

Respect your environment and it will reward you. Appreciate the opportunities the universe gives you to learn, to express and expand yourself every moment. If you criticize your medium of expression, you are demeaning yourself. Be grateful that it chose you. Allow life to express itself fully through you without blocking its flow with doubt, criticism, arrogance and resentment. Once you surrender, life flows through you joyfully.

No Ball

Arrogance. Ungratefulness. Thinking one is above the medium.

In the classic book *Zorba the Greek* by Nikos Kazantzakis, Zorba loves his medium of expression, specifically pottery on that occasion, and cuts off his finger because it was getting in the way. Extreme, one may say, but that is the extent one can go to. In the *Mahabharata*, we have the example of extreme devotion to the guru, when Ekalavya, the Nishadha Prince, cuts off his thumb and offers it as guru *dakshin*a to Drona, thereby giving up his dreams of being the world's greatest archer. It is an act of humility, to the guru and the medium, that should always be considered above oneself.

Dancers who pray to the stage as they step onto it, performers who touch the feet of their gurus each time they perform, soldiers who clean their weapons each day, they all show their humility and respect to the medium. Those who remained true to the process, refining and learning till the end, earned fame, name and respect, such as Bhimsen Joshi, MS Subbulakshmi, Gangubai Hangal and Balasaraswati among others.

I attended a concert by the Wadala Brothers a Chowmohalla Palace, Hyderabad. Their devotion to their art form, which is the purpose of their life, their wholesome gratitude at having been chosen to express it, draws you into the magic of that love affair. The words they use, the emotions they feel, the love in their eyes and the acts they do, touch you deeply.

The fascinating story of P Kalyana Sundaram of Tirunelveli, who gave away his entire life's earnings, pension benefits and even the prize attached to his 'Man of the Millennium' award, a considerable sum of ₹30 crore, for the benefit of the needy, whom he served all his life, comes to mind. To meet his own meager needs, the bachelor worked after school hours in a laundry facility nearby and other such small jobs. Kalyana Sundaram lived like that for over three decades now, serving the poor, while simultaneously doing a great job as a librarian at the college – he was recognized as the best librarian in India and was even ranked among the ten best librarians in the world. I have heard many other cases of poor people, modest people, giving up much of their meager earnings to the needy. It is humbling to hear such stories. They let life express itself through them, and it does in all its magnificence.

Bonus Runs

Humility keeps your path free to achieve greater things. It opens up wonderful new spaces.

Exercise: Write down all the reasons why you are the chosen one. What has the universe given you? How are you allowing it to express itself through you? What can you do to help it express itself more? Take your job. Write down all that it gives you. The opportunities it provides. Are you using all the opportunities it gives you? Is there something more you can do? Are you grateful? Practice gratitude and humility. You will grow.

---

47 | ROLE

"It is better to do one's duty, however defective it may be, than to follow the duty of another, however well one may perform it. He who does his duty as his own nature reveals it, never sins." – Lao Tzu

Know and perform your role.

IF EACH ONE OF US knew our role and performed it to the best of our ability, we'd achieve much as individuals and as a team. Instead, we do everything else but our role, underperform and interfere in everyone else's job. In cricket, good players understand and adapt to their roles. Opening batsmen are given a clear role of seeing off the dangerous new ball. Number three batsmen have the role of holding the innings together. New ball bowlers have the role of getting early breakthroughs. Cricketers perform specific roles as night watchmen, pinch hitters, change bowlers and so on. The 12th man and every single reserve in the team are given specific roles too. If any member of the team slacks off in their duty, it affects the team morale and performance. Such behaviour is not tolerated. Teams get the winning edge when all players perform their roles well and don't get into one another's way. Roles are spelt out in unambiguous terms in successful teams.

Key semifinal for IDBI against BPCL in a Times Shield game. I was struggling with an injured hamstring, but stayed on the field just in case my skipper needed me to bowl. The game was heading to a close finish. My friend Parag Paigankar was doing a great job from one end, but the other end was leaking runs. Our captain Jaideep Pal decided to risk me bowling my medium pace from a run up of a couple of steps. My role was clear – to keep one end tight, so Parag could attack. I focused on my role, kept it in the right areas and ended up picking three wickets. Though it was nothing extraordinary, I was proud of having performed the role assigned to me. I really enjoyed that performance, because we won.

Another time, I was assigned the role of being a reserve in a friendly match. Instead of performing my role, I gave some weak excuse and left the ground. Poor, unforgiveable behaviour.

Coach's Corner

Understand, define and perform your role to the best of your abilities. Know your boundaries. Even if it is lowly or seemingly unimportant, perform it as best as you can. Every role is interlinked to one another in a team. If everyone performs their role, team efficiency improves many times over.

No Ball

Roles that are not spelt out. Not knowing one's role. Not performing defined roles. Pointing fingers at others. Maverick ideas that endanger team effort. Trying to be the star, to show off and impress by going beyond one's role needlessly.

In Indian mythology, we hear the story of the elephant god Ganesha, who did not relinquish the duty his mother Goddess Parvathi entrusted him with. Let no one enter, Parvathi said, while she went for a bath and young Ganesha took his role with utmost seriousness. He denied entry to Lord Shiva himself, not knowing who he was and repulsed all the forces of Lord Shiva solidly. In the *Mahabharata*, young Abhimanyu performed a special role that only he could perform, even if it meant giving up his life.

My boss Mr Banerjee and I, prepared the presentation on the IT scenario in Andhra Pradesh. Our roles were cut out. Mr Banerjee was great at researching at presenting it and I was supposed to read out from the slides and keep it simple. But when I saw the audience, I decided to impress and went beyond my assigned role. I improvised, adlibbed and got badly stuck. Every time I tried to get out, I used something even more outrageous and dug a deeper hole for myself. It was a colossal disaster. I had no answer when my boss asked me good-naturedly why I deviated from my role and muffed it all up not just for me, but for my team. Never again. I should have stuck to my role.

Bonus Runs

When you know what is expected of you and live up to it, your performances are impactful. You can develop your role and make a greater impact on the team's result.

Exercise: Define your roles in all the teams that you are a part of – family, work, community, society. Write down how you can perform your role to the best of your capabilities. It will help your performance and that of your team's. You will be a valuable asset to any team.

---

48 | EQUALITY

"All men are created equal, it is only men themselves who place themselves above equality." –David Allan Coe

Everyone is equal in the team.

THERE ARE NO RACE, colour, caste, community, rich-poor or superior-inferior differences – everyone is out here to play for the team. The maharaja shares the same food, the same room and the same toilet as the poorest man. The only thing that counts is how they can play, individually and as a unit, not where they come from. The son of a wealthy man may have to serve drinks to the son of a chauffeur and no one feels the worse for it in a team. Cricket also equalizes in other ways – the one who got a 100 in the last game may get out for a duck today, the champion team of yesterday may get knocked out in the first round tomorrow.

The Mumbai Ranji cricket team, which won the Ranji Trophy more times than any other team, does not make any extra concessions to its stars, a culture that persisted right through the days of Sunil Gavaskar, Dilip Vengsarkar, Sandeep Patil and Ravi Shastri and percolated down to the era of Sachin Tendulkar, who in exemplary fashion, played for Mumbai in its Ranji win in his last year of first-class cricket. Vijay Mohan Raj, who played for Bombay, recalls how a Test player like Eknath Solkar would serve drinks when he was not playing. In his book *Bombay Boys*, Makarand Waingankar profiles players who were rich and poor, from all communities and castes. All that mattered was the team performance. So ingrained is the culture of equality in such teams. No wonder Mumbai is the toughest team to beat in Indian domestic cricket.

The Osmania University College of Business Management's Cricket Team of 1991 comprised of two regular cricketers, many small time cricketers, two badminton players, one basketball player and a taekwondo champion. No one gave our motley crowd a chance of going beyond the first round of the inter-collegiate tournament, but we were a close-knit bunch who ate together, played together and stayed together as equals. When we played, everyone in our college (our extended family) turned up to support us. Against all odds, we made it to the final of the inter-collegiate tournament. We had an

equal part – players and supporters. Never underestimate the
power of synergy in team games.

Coach's Corner

When all members of the team are equal, the team comes together powerfully like a fist. When teams come together, they are most effective. No one is greater or lesser, everyone is equally important. As teams bond, everyone stands up for one another and greater synergies are achieved.

No Ball

Disruptive elements. Egoists. Those who feel they don't need to fit in. If they don't fit in, they are best removed from the team.

Racism, casteism and communalism have divided Team Humanity always. The thought that one is superior to another has eaten away the core of Team Humanity. Despite all the wise men preaching equality and unity, the hubris of being better than another has cost us dear. Humans have created inequalities based on region, religion, colour, community, faith, belief, culture and caste among other things and propagated the false belief that some are superior to others.

Dr Bhim Rao Ambedkar, born into an untouchable Mahar family, would have been relegated to menial jobs assigned to his caste if he had not been empowered with one equalizer – education. The untouchable castes were until then not allowed to draw water from wells, because they were considered impure people, were not allowed to touch those belonging to higher castes, to go to schools or celebrate functions and follow certain customs that higher castes did. But given one opportunity, Ambedkar studied in school, sitting apart from the rest of the class on a gunny sack and not drinking water on days when the school peon was not present, because he was not allowed to. He became the first untouchable to graduate from Bombay University, did a doctorate from Columbia University, is known as the 'Father of the Indian Constitution' and was independent India's first law minister. Given half a chance to be treated equally, the untouchable who was kept away shone bright and proved that his wisdom, vision and intelligence were second to none. One equalizer was all he needed.

Adolf Hitler, whose hatred for non-whites and Jews was well known, predicted that the 1936 Berlin Olympics would showcase the dominance of the Aryan race. Carl Ludwig Long, a German athlete and a medal hopeful in the 1936 Olympic Games in Berlin, was competing against

African American legend Jesse Owens in the long jump. Owens fouled two of his jumps and was under pressure to get his third and final jump right to qualify (which would have been in Long's favour), but Long put such petty thoughts aside, went to Owens and gave him sound advice to jump from well behind the line, because he would qualify even then. Owens took his advice, qualified and went on to win the gold in long jump, while Long won the silver. Long went even further. He was the first to congratulate Owens, embraced him, walked round the stadium with him and posed for pictures.

I remember two young boys of 11 and 12 coming to the coaching camp where I coached. One was the son of a chauffeur and the other the son of a wealthy professional. After many years, I saw them both again recently, handsome and strong as young teenagers, sharing the easy friendship that they always had. Cricket as they say, is a great equalizer in more ways than one.

Bonus Runs

When you get it across that everyone in the team is equally important, you form a strong, united team that performs as a resilient unit.

Exercise: Get your team members to share their career and life aspirations. Let them share their fears, doubts, loves, hates, strengths, weaknesses and histories with one another. It helps them get closer and understand one another better once they know that inside we are all the same. Watch how the energy changes in the team. You will find it so much easier to relate to everyone.

49 | RESPECT

"There is no greater danger than to underestimate your opponent." – Lao Tzu.

Never underestimate the opponent.

TO RESPECT THE OPPONENT is to be aware. The West Indies team that won the 1975 and 1979 versions of the World Cup was high on confidence as it ran into a lowly ranked India in the final of the 1983 World Cup. Malcolm Marshall reportedly booked a BMW car that he planned to pay for with his winnings from the finals. One can well imagine how the mighty Windies might have taken victory for granted after India managed only 183 in its innings. The greats played careless shots, hoped that they could still get by, and before they realized it, paid a heavy price for underestimating the opponent.

Bangladesh beat Australia, Kenya beat West Indies, Ireland beat Australia – each one a case of the stronger and more fancied teams paying dearly for underestimating the opponent. The message is clear – underestimate the opponent at your own peril. To give a flicker of hope to the opponent is to give rise to a demon that devours you. Treat every opponent with the greatest respect.

The press in Calicut hailed the Osmania team as the favourites to win the South Zone Universities Championships in 1985. Our team arrived with eight Ranji Trophy probables in our team. The University management had booked tickets for the All India Rohinton Baria trophy that is played by the winners and runners of each Zone. As a result, before the first game with Bharathiyar University had begun, we were already looking beyond the final. Our prophecies seemed on track when, chasing our total of 245, their main batsman and my good friend VB Chandrasekhar, got out first ball, lofting me high into the skies where mid off caught a steepler. As they collapsed to 65 for 5 in 18 overs, our overconfidence combined dangerously with a gross underestimation of our rivals. The next pair scored 180 runs and took Bharathiyar to victory with five overs to spare. It was by far the most humiliating defeat we suffered and one that we will carry forever in our hearts. Never ever underestimate anyone. (Never make early bookings.)

Coach's corner

Take up every job with utmost respect. Never underestimate anyone. Watch out for the parts where you feel overconfident, where you think you can take it easy. Those oversights will come back to haunt you. Underestimating the small clauses could cost you dearly. There is no such thing as an easy job or a weak enemy. Inculcate a healthy respect for every competitor, every job. Make that a practice. There will be no upsets.

No Ball

Overconfidence. Taking things for granted. Disrespecting people.

The good old rabbit found this principle out when he lost to the determined tortoise in a race. A nap? What was the rabbit thinking? Haven't we seen many such rabbits on the world stage? And they learnt costly lessons in the past too. But still, the rabbits of the world continue down that path, picking on seemingly weak enemies that they think they can push over. In all cases, they end up paying a big price. Too bad that some of the world powers don't play cricket – this is one lesson that cricket teaches pretty fast.

Hollywood superstars Dustin Hoffman and Gene Hackman were both voted as the ones who were least expected to make it big in their acting class. In fact, when Gene Hackman was struggling to make ends meet and was working as a doorman at a restaurant, he bumped into one of his teachers who told him that he knew he would come to no good as an actor. A little prematurely one would think. Both the actors became acting powerhouses and superstars and won many awards, including two Academy Awards each. You do not want to underestimate anyone.

Vincent van Gogh, one of the most famous painters in history, was a relative unknown at the time of his death as few people knew his work and appreciated it. Van Gogh, however, kept at it, painting over 2,100 art works, of 860 oil paintings and 1,300 water colours. Today, Van Gogh's paintings are among the most expensive and some sell for over USD 100 million. For all those who never cared two hoots for the man when he was alive, it must have come as a rude shock.

Bonus Runs

When you respect opponents and the medium, you come well prepared and do justice to your ability and ranking. There will be no unexpected surprises.

Exercise: Identify the issues in your life that are showing small signs of wear and tear. Don't let the small issues grow bigger than they should. Address them when they are small and resolve them, else they will come back and haunt you later. Never underestimate the small issues.

Look at your opponents. See what you respect in them. Is it possible to emulate those aspects? Every opponent will teach you something so be open to learn from the good they do or even the mistakes they make. Respect them for that and for making you a better person or player.

50 | FAIRNESS

"Fairness is not an attitude. It's a professional skill that must be developed and exercised." – Brit Hume

It's just not cricket.

BEING SPORTIVE IS DOING the right thing – it's the only thing that counts in the end. It reflects what one has learned from sports. Much of the way cricket, or for that matter any sport, is played is about fairness. It is not uncommon to see cricketers check with the opposition team members whether they had taken a catch cleanly or edged a ball, and trusting their word for it. Similarly, cricketers give the benefit of doubt and trust opposition scorers, pitches, umpires, sometimes even helping the opposition by fielding for them. Laws are viewed leniently by cricketers, taking into account the intent of the act in a run out, in taking or not taking overthrows and handling the ball or injury.

Unfair tactics range from claiming wickets and runs unfairly, taking unfair advantage in a situation, interpreting a law or rule unfairly, cheating, doctoring score sheets, wickets, selections, tampering with balls and equipment to more forceful methods, such as coercing, obstructing the field, threatening and even beating up players and umpires, bribing umpires, etc. All of these are frowned upon. It's just not cricket.

Indian Test captains Gundappa Vishwanath and MS Dhoni recalled opponent batsmen on the biggest stage, after the batsmen had been adjudged out by the umpires. Vishwanath recalled Bob Taylor of England in the Jubilee Test played in February 1980. England was in dire straits at 58 for 5 then and Taylor was adjudged caught behind off Kapil Dev. Vishwanath checked with the batsman Taylor whether he had nicked the ball and when Taylor said he had not, he recalled him and asked him to bat on. Indian skipper MS Dhoni withdrew his appeal and recalled England's Ian Bell, who was run out in the 2nd Test at Trent Bridge in the 2011 Test series between India and England. On both occasions, the batsmen had been adjudged out by the umpires.

Our number three batsman Suri was freakishly run out on 99,
but the rule in our team was clear – no adding one run from
extras, etc. to make up the 100. After the match, a bunch of
our teammates approached me without his knowledge. Why
don't we add that one single in the score sheet? It could help
his selection and the opposition would not mind. I explained
to them that such shortcuts will not help. Let Suri enjoy the
pride of having scored 99, not the shame of having cheated for
one extra run. Why demean his grand effort by adding that
run? The issue never came up again. In fact, when playing
for MCC, we lost close games, but never fudged score sheets,
never picked fights with umpires and the opposition, gave
our equipment and players on loan to opposition and did our
bit to help the game proceed fairly. Not that we were aiming
for sainthood, but we believed we could win fair and square.
Also, the history of the club weighed heavily on us – many
internationals had played for it. It was no wonder that many
opposition teams looked forward to the prospect of a good
game of cricket with us.

Coach's Corner

Do unto others what you expect them to do to you in the
same situation. Fairness is what we expect of one another
as humans. Playing fair indicates that you are secure as a
person and do not need any untoward advantage. When

you resort to unfair means, it indicates a lack of confidence in your ability to win on your own. Act with responsibility.

No Ball

Unfair behaviour. Greedy behaviour. End justifying the means.

Arsenal Football Club, a premier football club based in London, offered and played a rematch against Sheffield United in 1999 after it won, because Arsenal felt they had taken an unfair advantage through a misunderstanding. Fair play at its best one would say. On an individual level, footballer Paulo Di Canio did not shoot at an open goal when he noticed the Everton goal keeper Paul Gerrard lying on the ground. In another sport, Eugenio Monte, the Italian bob sled champion, leading the race, gave Briton Tony Nash a bolt from his own bobsled to fix his bobsled. Nash won the gold. Fairness exists in the biggest stages, where the biggest stakes are won or lost.

In the movie *Fearless* (2006), the final fight between Jet Li's character (based on real-life martial arts expert Huo Yuanjia) and the Japanese fighter Tanaka, showcases a wonderful example of fairness. In the final fight, Huo Yuanjia is asked to fight four fighters in one day, one after another. He defeats the first three and is ready to take on Tanaka, who is the fourth, but fair-minded Tanaka declares that the fight is unfair and that he does not mind waiting until the next day to fight Huo. Even after the fight starts, Tanaka repeatedly makes the offer to stop the fight when he notices that Huo is not well. A true sportsman fights fair and square. Tanaka would have won a Fairplay award hands down in any century, any sport.

Bonus Runs

Playing fair fosters an environment of mutual respect, trust and healthy competition. You get what you give.

Exercise: Think of the times when you stepped over the line and took an unfair stand. Then reflect on the times when you restrained yourself and took a fair stand. Compare how you felt in both situations. How would you like to do things now? Take the fair route. You will find it hugely liberating and beneficial to your growth.

JAICO PUBLISHING HOUSE

Elevate Your Life. Transform Your World.

ESTABLISHED IN 1946, Jaico Publishing House is home to world-transforming authors such as Sri Sri Paramahansa Yogananda, Osho, The Dalai Lama, Sri Sri Ravi Shankar, Sadhguru, Robin Sharma, Deepak Chopra, Jack Canfield, Eknath Easwaran, Devdutt Pattanaik, Khushwant Singh, John Maxwell, Brian Tracy and Stephen Hawking.

Our late founder Mr. Jaman Shah first established Jaico as a book distribution company. Sensing that independence was around the corner, he aptly named his company Jaico ('Jai' means victory in Hindi). In order to service the significant demand for affordable books in a developing nation, Mr. Shah initiated Jaico's own publications. Jaico was India's first publisher of paperback books in the English language.

While self-help, religion and philosophy, mind/body/spirit, and business titles form the cornerstone of our non-fiction list, we publish an exciting range of travel, current affairs, biography, and popular science books as well. Our renewed focus on popular fiction is evident in our new titles by a host of fresh young talent from India and abroad. Jaico's recently established Translations Division translates selected English content into nine regional languages.

Jaico's Higher Education Division (HED) is recognized for its student-friendly textbooks in Business Management and Engineering which are in use countrywide.

In addition to being a publisher and distributor of its own titles, Jaico is a major national distributor of books of leading international and Indian publishers. With its headquarters in Mumbai, Jaico has branches and sales offices in Ahmedabad, Bangalore, Bhopal, Bhubaneswar, Chennai, Delhi, Hyderabad, Kolkata and Lucknow.

SINCE 1946